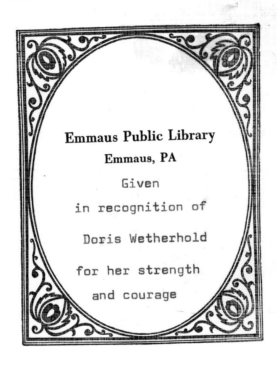

WINNIN
LIFE'S
TOUGH
BATTLE

Other books by Julius Segal:

SLEEP (with Gay Gaer Luce)

INSOMNIA (with Gay Gaer Luce)

A CHILD'S JOURNEY (with Herbert Yahraes)

GROWING UP SMART & HAPPY (with Zelda Segal)

PSYCHOLOGY: AN INTRODUCTION (with Jerome Kagan and Ernest Havemann)

WINNING LIFE'S TOUGHEST BATTLES

Roots of Human Resilience

DR. JULIUS SEGAL

MCGRAW-HILL BOOK COMPANY
New York   St. Louis   San Francisco
Hamburg   Mexico   Toronto

1 2 3 4 5 6 7 8 9 D O C D O C 8 7 6

ISBN 0-07-056034-X

LIBRARY OF CONGRESS CATALOGING-IN-PUBLICATION DATA

Segal, Julius, 1924–
  Winning life's toughest battles.
  Includes bibliographical references and index.
  1. Conduct of life.   2. Consolation.   I. Title.
BJ1581.2.S4258   1986   155.9   86-116
ISBN 0-07-056034-X

Book design by Beth Tondreau

To Zelda

Contents

Contents

CONTENTS

Preface

This book is about the ways we can surmount the overwhelming crises of our lives. It is about how we can live through and conquer the stresses we suffer when a loved one dies, a marriage crumbles, a career is ruined, disease strikes, life savings disappear. It is about people who have successfully endured personal disasters—crippling accidents, rape, life-threatening illness. It is about triumphant victims of the unspeakable trauma of captivity—hostages and POWs—whose experiences can teach us all how to live victoriously despite our own adversities.

Some of the people you will be reading about in this book have endured crises that may at first seem far removed from your own life. Most of us, for example, will never suffer rape, or be taken captive. Yet at one time or another, each of us must confront stresses that challenge our individual capacity to endure. For some, it may be illness, or crushing financial reverses; for others, the anguish of family discord, a child gone astray, or bereavement; for still others, the pain of loss—of a loving relationship, a job, or well-being. Crises and trauma are facts of life, and there are precious lessons to be learned from those who have been challenged to the very limit—and triumphed.

I am talking here about the real thing—surviving catastrophic events—and not about handling the everyday irritants of life. This book does not teach the relaxation techniques—breathing exercises, mantras and meditations, biofeedback—that you can practice when work gets out of hand, you misplace your wallet, or the car won't start. Plenty of advice is already available to help us unwind, hang loose, and fight off that tension headache. This is not such a book. It is about strategies for living—not tactics for getting by.

In writing this book, I have drawn in part on my studies of men and women who have experienced the searing ordeal of captivity—certainly one of the most traumatic experiences life can hold. In 1954, I conducted the U.S. Army's official analysis of the more than 3,000 POWs returned from "brainwashing" in Korea. Twenty years later, I joined a small group of Navy psychiatrists and psychologists asked to assist in the reentry of those 550 men who lived through an incredible nightmare as captives in Vietnam. More recently, I served as a member of the State Department task force charged with helping the 52 hostages released after fourteen months of incarceration in Iran. And over the decades since World War II, I have studied the fate of concentration camp survivors—men and women who escaped the Nazi death ovens and created new lives and families in the United States, Europe, and Israel.

This book draws as well on the results of research on victorious survivors who rarely make the headlines—parents of cancer-ridden children, targets of rape and assault, victims of crippling accidents and deadly diseases. I have also described my experiences in working with refugees, torn from their homelands and cast adrift in a strange new world, who have nevertheless prevailed over their circumstances. And finally, I have shared my own personal confrontations with crises—devastating illness, the death of family, the threatened destruction of my career.

Despite the subject matter, this book is not somber. Although it describes pain and loss, its theme is inspiration and hope— for it shows how surprisingly resilient and adaptable we actually are. Throughout, the reader will find demonstrations of the incredible range of human endurance. Using lessons from the lives of triumphant survivors, this book teaches us how we, too, can work through and conquer the crises all of us are bound to encounter in our own lives.

A list of references to studies and other published sources cited in the book is provided at the end. The references are arranged alphabetically, by chapter.

The task of producing this book was completed with financial support provided by Patricia van A. Kind, the William T. Grant Foundation, and the Maurice Falk Medical Fund. I am deeply grateful to Mrs. Kind, Robert J. Haggerty, M.D., and Philip B. Hallen for their generous encouragement and assistance.

Julius Segal
Bethesda, Md.

WINNING LIFE'S TOUGHEST BATTLES

We're like tea bags. We don't know our own
strength until we get into hot water.
BRUCE LAINGEN,
former hostage in Iran

Introduction:
How Resilient
are You?

"**Y**ou are a hostage!"

With these words, hissed in his ear by an Iranian terrorist, a
proud American foreign-service officer suddenly became a powerless captive. Blindfolded, the barrel of a gun at his temple, he
entered the hell of captivity along with Bruce Laingen and 63
others.

Although some would soon be released, 444 days would pass
before this bewildered hostage came home. During that time,
he would face long and brutal interrogations, often throughout
the night. He would spend nearly 150 days in isolation, in a tiny
cell containing only a foul mattress—home for an army of cen-
tipedes that marched across his face whenever he tried to sleep.

No word from his family was allowed to reach him, and his
existence was so cruelly regimented that he could urinate only

1

with special permission. His relentless dysentery went untreated, and he shed a pound for every week of his captivity.

In the stillness of one hot summer night, the hostage was blindfolded, stripped to his undershorts, and led outside for execution. He heard the cocking of the rifles ("I was praying the end would come quickly," he remembers), but the triggers were never pulled. Small wonder that "every day thereafter, the presence of death was on my mind."

According to popular expectations, this man should have become the victim of lifelong emotional problems. For months prior to his release, pundits and professionals alike offered dire predictions of the outcome for our captives in Tehran. Unhealable scars would blemish their psyches, we were told, and they would remain emotional and physical wrecks for the rest of their lives. One psychologist, later taken to task for her remarks by the American Psychological Association, announced her mournful prognoses on national television: ". . . permanent problems in interpersonal relationships . . . permanent coordination difficulties . . . permanent damage to memory."

No such forecasts have been realized. Like most of his comrades, the hostage emerged to freedom without lingering symptoms: no disabling anxiety or depression, no lacerating guilt, no insuperable problems readapting to the world he had left behind. Instead, he quickly regained his vigor, picked up the threads of his family life, and resumed his diplomatic career. Today, more than five years later, he is a leader in his community, and his mental health continues to be excellent.

This case is not unique. For over three decades, I have studied victims of overwhelming stress—concentration camp survivors, POWs liberated from years of captivity, terrorized hostages, bewildered refugees, and victims of such trauma as rape, abuse, bereavement, financial disaster, and spoiled careers. Repeatedly, I have been inspired by the countless cases that run counter to "expert" predictions. Instead of a pattern of deficit and defeat, there is one of coping and conquest. Indeed, rather than being devastated by their suffering, many survivors have actually used the experience to enrich their lives.

How Much Can a Person Take?

Consider these three cases:

- At age twenty-three, Everett Alvarez was the first American airman to be taken prisoner in North Vietnam. He spent almost a decade of his life in POW prisons, often in brutal solitary confinement. For months on end, the scurrying of huge rats in his cell was the only sound he heard. His daily ration often consisted of a chicken head floating in grease. At times he was afflicted with severe intestinal disorders. Uncontrollable diarrhea and high fevers dehydrated and emaciated him. After his sixth year as a POW, his captors gleefully delivered a devastating letter from his mother: Alvarez's wife had decided not to wait for his return; she had found another man. For Everett now, there was not only no present but no future either.

- As a young adolescent, Susan Salasin was brutally attacked by an assailant who left her physically disfigured and psychologically ravaged. For months she went through what seemed like endless operations to reassemble her shattered face. The prospect of returning home and resuming school aroused unspeakable dread.

- Frances Hardy is a widow—twice over. After six years of happy marriage, her first husband died a slow death from a ravaging cancer that spread from his testicles to his brain. A few years later, she married again. But after three contented years, she watched a drunken driver run down her husband as he crossed the street to join her for lunch.

According to popular and professional wisdom, these three victims should never have recovered. To be sure, all three endured for a time the painful reactions that naturally follow such trauma. But psychologically crippled? Hardly. Indeed, in some ways they, too, were ultimately strengthened by their trials.

Everett Alvarez, now remarried, lives with his devoted wife and two handsome sons outside Washington, D.C. Recently graduated from law school, he serves as deputy administrator of the Veterans Administration. He is a contented and beloved husband and father.

Susan Salasin returned to school, picked up the pieces of her life, and went on to college. Today, at forty-five, she is a loving wife and mother—and, for nearly ten years, the head of a national program to assist victims of precisely the kind of crime she endured.

Frances Hardy returned to her long-interrupted schooling and eventually earned a degree in computer science. Then she moved to California, starting a fresh life among new friends and surroundings, her double-barreled trauma a manageable memory of "my previous existence."

How do such victims avoid the anticipated disastrous effects of their ordeals? What is it that allows them to ultimately survive, strong and whole, despite crushing misfortune?

The answers, of course, are varied. Each person has a unique coping style. Yet in the triumphs of these survivors—and many more like them—there are basic lessons for all of us. First, however, let us examine the surprisingly diverse events that can challenge the ability of any one of us to endure.

The Varieties of Life Crises

No life is without traumas. Eventually we must all confront events that test our limits. "There are many ways to be a victim," writes University of Illinois psychologist Joseph E. McGrath, whose inventory includes those who suffer a serious accident or contract a deadly disease; people who are assaulted, raped, robbed, or abducted; and those who find themselves in the path of such catastrophes as tornadoes, hurricanes, earthquakes, fires, or floods. For some of us, it may be chronic illness; for others, the loss of a job or crushing financial reverses; for still others the torment of having a sick or emotionally disturbed child. In the words of renowned psychologist Carl Rogers, "It's an awfully risky thing to live."

Many of us find it terrifying to acknowledge that we ourselves may ever become victims. We imagine that traumatic crises occur only in other people's lives, never in our own. Psychologist Linda S. Perloff calls this our "illusions of invulnerability." Sooner or later, however, reality overtakes us.

The next time you are in a group, try this experiment: Ask the others to think as hard as they can and decide whether they have recently felt themselves to be among life's victims. You may be surprised at the results, as I was one day during a meeting of mental health professionals.

Two dozen of us—a group known as the State Department Interagency Task Force—met regularly during the Iran hostage crisis to plan how we could best offer psychological help to the hostages when they were finally released. From the start, however, we admitted a problem: Hard though we tried, we found it difficult to put ourselves in the hostages' place—to feel, deep in our guts, what their experience of captivity might actually be like. Then one day a member of our group asked us to think: Were our lives *really* so far removed from those of the hostages? How many of us had recently had cause to regard ourselves as victims?

As it turned out, nearly all of us had recently felt threatened or exploited. The actual episodes reported by the group members differed widely. One social worker had been the victim of a break-in. A psychologist had lost his younger sister to leukemia. And a psychiatrist had learned of his wife's plans to leave him. The result of our collective realization was dramatic. We felt a powerful surge of empathy toward the 52 captives, held for over a year, whom we would soon be welcoming back.

This experiment, showing the surprising variety of our experiences with stress, raises a perplexing question: How traumatic does a particular episode actually have to be to qualify as a crisis? What does it take to reduce a person to the status of victim?

To help answer the question, one team of investigators assigned a numerical value to the crises we encounter during the course of our lives. After studying the life experiences of large numbers of people, U.S. Navy physician-researchers Thomas H. Holmes and Richard H. Rahe developed a widely used "Life Stress Scale" that gives scores to difficult turning points in life, including positive as well as negative happenings such as marriage and bereavement.

Heading the list of negative events on the Holmes–Rahe scale is the death of a spouse, which gets a full 100 points. Also included are such crises as divorce, separation, imprisonment, the loss of a close family member, being fired, and the death of a dear friend—each of which has a different numerical weight. The likelihood of bodily breakdown, the investigators found, is determined by the total numerical value of the stresses endured during a twelve-month period. When the number exceeded 200, more than half of the people in their study became physically ill.

The problem with such an accounting, however, is that it leaves no room for the personal and often unique perceptions we have of the various crises we may confront during our lives. There are, in other words, surprising disparities in the way we perceive our troubles. In this book you will read about experiences that some people find excruciatingly difficult to deal with, while others do not.

To be sure, most of us would agree that some experiences are more devastating than others. A stolen car, for example, is hardly as serious as an incurable cancer. University of London psychiatrist Michael Rutter has described three kinds of life events that appear to be especially painful: events that mean the loss of an important relationship—for example, divorce; events that cannot be controlled and therefore produce a feeling of helplessness—for example, an accident; and events that have lasting consequences—for example, a lingering illness or the loss of a job.

Still, the impact of any particular crisis can vary dramatically from one person to the next. One individual fired from a job, for example, may buoyantly set out to find a new one—or even to start a new career; another may withdraw from the stress and seize the opportunity to take a long-postponed vacation; and a third may begin to experience severe anxiety and depression.

In *The Crime Victim's Book*, psychologist Morton Bard and writer Dawn Sangrey report that the same is true of victims of various personal crimes: "The degree of violation experienced by an individual victim finally depends on the meaning of the crime in that person's life. What seems a minor incident to one victim may be a personal catastrophe for another." Our subjective appraisal of a stressful event determines how traumatic that event actually turns out to be. The poet Percy Bysshe Shelley put it best: "Grief is a matter of relativity; the sorrow should be estimated by its proportion to the sorrower; a gash is as painful to one as an amputation is to another."

This book is addressed to you if you feel wounded by stress—or recognize that you may one day be—for whatever reason. In the pages that follow, you will be reading about people whose traumatic experiences may at first seem remote from your own.

But by the time you finish this book, you will see that however varied the crises we encounter in life, and however differently we may perceive them, one or another of them is likely one day to make us doubt our capacity to endure.

Our Hidden Power to Overcome

"I should like this to be accepted as my confession," wrote the poet Katherine Mansfield in her book *Journal* shortly before she died in 1922. "There is no limit to human suffering. When one thinks, 'Now I have touched the bottom of the sea—now I can go no deeper,' one goes deeper . . . I do not want to die without leaving a record of my belief that suffering can be overcome."

Many of us believe the opposite. Captain Richard A. Stratton, now director of the Naval Academy Preparatory School in Newport, Rhode Island, lived through six savage years as a POW in Vietnam. Stratton has spoken to thousands of groups since his return from captivity. "In every group," says Stratton, "there is an unspoken question in the minds of my listeners. 'I wonder if I could do it.' And the silent answer is: 'I don't think I could.' "

"People say to me," observes Alvarez, "that they don't know how I did it. 'Gosh,' they say, 'I never could have gone through those eight and a half years.' And I say to them, 'If I could do it, you could, too.' People just don't give themselves enough credit." Concludes former hostage Bruce Laingen: "We're like tea bags. We don't know our own strength until we get into hot water."

As a psychologist, I admit that my own profession has been largely responsible for our self-defeating tendency to live scared, to expect to crumble in the face of crisis rather than to surmount it. For many decades, psychologists have concentrated their efforts on trying to learn why some people break down under stress, not on how they might overcome it. We have directed our energies, says University of Minnesota psychologist Norman Garmezy, to "the study of patterns of maladaptation and incompetence." The reason, he says, is that "our mental health practitioners and researchers are predisposed by interest, investment, and training in seeing deviance, psychopathology, and weakness wherever they look." All but ignored have been the vast number of people—most of us, I believe—who, when armed with the right coping techniques, are able to endure and to live triumphantly despite crushing stress. Indeed, until recently, the human capacity for conquering life crises appears to have been one of psychology's best-kept secrets.

I do not deny, of course, that stress has the potential to do us harm. Researchers have carefully detailed how disturbing life events can leave a residue of "post-traumatic stress" symptoms—psychological problems such as anxiety, irritability, depression, and nightmares, or one or another of a vast array of physical ailments that include high blood pressure, heart attacks, bronchial asthma, colitis, and stomach ulcers.

I did not write this book to refute the existence of such symptoms—or the fact that some of them can plague trauma victims for years. But I do reject the assumption made by many mental health professionals that such problems are inevitable or universal—that they are penalties we must all pay. Even studies of concentration camp survivors—the ultimate "victims"—show that, contrary to popular assumption, many have adapted surprisingly well in the years beyond their ordeal. The findings of a recent study of Holocaust survivors now living in Montreal, for example, focus attention on what the authors describe as "the magnificent ability of human beings to rebuild shattered lives, careers, and families, even as they wrestle with the bitterest of memories."

This book will demonstrate that buried in all of us are undreamed-of powers of healing and growth in the face of stress. The testimony of the survivors described here is clear enough:

We are rarely as fragile as we imagine ourselves to be. The pages that follow will offer living proof of the incredible coping skills all of us have.

A tantalizing enigma remains, however. What is it that separates the copers from the casualties—those who survive from those who do not? How do they avoid the anticipated effects of their ordeal? What is it that allows them not only to endure but to live productively? Most important: What can we ourselves learn from the victors, and apply in our own lives?

That is what the rest of this book is about.

Give sorrow words: the grief that does not
speak, whispers in the over-wrought heart and
bids it break.
WILLIAM SHAKESPEARE
Macbeth

1.
Communication: Lifeline for Survival

"I would not be here today," a recovered cancer patient recently told me, "if I hadn't called my favorite cousin for a talk whenever I felt overwhelmed."

"Every few days, I used to meet Tom for lunch, and just telling him about my struggle gave me the guts to go on." These are the words of a former alcoholic whose family and career nearly collapsed in ruins.

Many people who have successfully weathered staggering crises echo the same theme. Communication—even with only one person—offered them a lifeline for survival. Unfortunately, the natural activity of human communication is not always easy in the face of crushing stress. At crisis points in our lives, we often feel strangely remote and disengaged from friends and even family. At such times we grow convinced that we are suffering alone—

that no one else could possibly care or understand—and the tendency to withdraw is therefore strong.

"Everything I said to anyone seemed flat and pointless. I wanted to sleep, to disappear somehow. Every night when I went to bed I prayed that I would never have to see or speak to anyone again." So a mother described how she felt when her fifteen-year-old son was killed one summer evening while riding his bicycle. Her words make vivid the impulse felt by many of us to break off all ties with those around us when we are under severe trauma.

The lessons from survivors teach us otherwise. Communication is essential, observed British social philosopher Sir Geoffrey Vickers, "to make personal experience bearable." Few individuals can cope with trauma alone. Even the most powerful figures in the world need contact with others in the face of crisis. In November 1963, following the shock and tragedy of President Kennedy's assassination, the new president, Lyndon B. Johnson, kept his close friend Horace Busby at his bedside until two in the morning after his first grueling day in office.

Probably no human beings have learned to recognize the importance of communication better than those who have successfully endured captivity.

Communicating from the Depths

Few captives ever suffered more than Vice Admiral James B. Stockdale, a heroic survivor of 2,714 days as a POW in Vietnam. On one occasion, the North Vietnamese handcuffed Stockdale's hands behind his back, locked his legs in heavy irons, and dragged him from his dark prison cell to sit in an unshaded courtyard so other prisoners could see what happened to anybody who refused to cooperate.

According to the Navy's official report of the episode, Stockdale remained in that position for three days. Since he had not been in the sun for a long time, he soon felt weak, but the guards would not let him sleep. He was beaten repeatedly. After one beating, Stockdale heard a towel snapping out in prison code the letters GBUJS. It was a message he would never forget: "God Bless You Jim Stockdale."

In every episode of captivity in recent American history, POWs and hostages have been sustained by ingeniously improvised lifelines of communication. In Vietnam, a clever tap code, in which the number and sequence of taps spelled out letters of the alphabet, became the prisoners' chief means of communication. It was this code that sustained Jim Stockdale.

At first the prisoners had trouble remembering the letter codes long enough to put them together to form coherent messages. Soon, however, their proficiency improved, and the system became second nature. The lonely prisoners tapped on the walls, the ceilings, or the floor. For short distances, they tapped with their fingers; for longer ones, they used their fists, elbows, or tin cups. "Soon enough," remembers Alvarez, "message traffic was flowing from one cell block to another, then even from building to building."

Eventually the POWs developed sophisticated extensions of the tapping routine. An especially effective ploy was to sweep through a prison compound using the broom movement to "talk" to an entire group. If one man walked by another's cell, he could drag his sandals in code. Some men sent messages to their comrades through the noises they made while shaking out their blankets, others by belching, blowing their noses, or, for a few prisoners who had the talent to do so at will, passing gas. One POW feigned sleep for a couple of hours each day during the siesta period and through his snoring managed to report how everyone was doing and what was going on in his cellblock.

Even body scratching—common in prison compounds—became a means of communication. One prisoner under heavy pressure to make an anti-American statement knew that as he passed through an empty courtyard on his way to the bath area many American eyes would be riveted on him, wanting to know whether he had been able to hold out. So he would scratch out the letter "c," then the letter "o," then the letter "p," and so on until he had scratched out the precious word: "c-o-p-i-n-g." After five and a half years, much of it in solitary confinement, Navy Lieutenant Commander John S. McCain III concluded that "the most important thing for survival as a POW was communication with someone, even if it was only a wave or a wink, a tap on a wall, or to have a guy put his thumb up. It made all the difference."

Lieutenant Commander Robert Shumaker, one of the first POWs taken in Vietnam, was convinced that he could endure what lay ahead if only he were able to make contact with a comrade. He managed to find a few dry ink spots in his cell and revived them with drops of water. Using matchsticks as pens, he put a message on a piece of toilet paper. The note simply asked the recipient's name, and it revealed places in the latrine where cement or bricks were loose and notes could be hidden.

Eventually Shumaker became aware that another prisoner had arrived in camp. He rolled up his note until it was not larger than a pencil eraser, and on his next visit to the latrine he hid it beneath a loose scrap of cement. On a piece of toilet paper he scrawled the words "Take me," placing it next to the privy hole. Then he waited.

"On his next visit to the latrine," writes John G. Hubbell in his book, *P. O. W.: A Definitive History of the American Prisoner of War Experience*, "Shumaker found his note missing. In place of the one he had hidden he found another, scratched onto a piece of toilet paper with the charcoaled end of a matchstick. It said simply: 'Storz, Capt., USAF.' Shumaker could not recall ever having been so elated."

14

Throughout their long ordeal, our POWs in Vietnam never yielded in their struggle to stay in touch with one another, even against seemingly impossible odds. They even used their excrement as a vehicle. "We made little boats out of paper containing messages and then floated them in our waste," former POW Stratton recalled when I talked to him recently. "We did our business in a little bucket, and one guy would collect it for the whole cellblock and dump it in the latrine. But first he would safely extract the precious notes. We all knew that our captors would never bother to pick up or inspect our manure."

What was so critical about staying in touch? The messages prisoners sent to one another breached their mounting loneliness and despair, and gave them the strength to survive. "They were," says former POW Everett Alvarez, "acts of self-healing. We really got to know each other through our silent conversations across the brick walls. Eventually, we learned all about each other's childhood, background, experiences, wives and children, hopes and ambitions." Says Stockdale: "It was a way of linking our lives and dreams together."

Katherine Koob agrees. In Tehran, she and hostage Ann Swift were blindfolded each morning and escorted to the bathroom. Left alone inside, they would pick through the wastebasket for possible clues about fellow hostages, looking for scraps of letters or notes. They even tried to count how many plates were being scraped after hostages being held nearby finished their meal, or to tally the number of chicken bones in the trash.

Eventually Koob and Swift persuaded their captors to allow them to cook for six other hostages being held in the same building. They never actually saw the beneficiaries of their culinary efforts, but the notes they managed to recover allowed them to feel "in touch."

The notes contained not only "compliments to the chef," but requests for future dishes. "Some peanut butter cookies would taste good if you've got the peanut butter," read one. "We'd love to get some lettuce," said another. The furtive messages were signed by "The Boys in the Back Room." Said Koob on her return to freedom: "Just knowing that someone in the next cell cared that I existed helped me go on."

Throughout the months of their captivity, our hostages in Iran kept despair at bay by staying in contact and giving one another comfort even when they could not speak. Some of them actually met for the first time when they were finally liberated. Yet they felt as if they had known one another through their covert communications across the prison barriers that separated them in Tehran. Despite their isolation, they had developed a support network that saw them through their ordeal—the kind all of us need if we are to survive the crises in our own lives.

Social Supports: The Ties That Bind— and Heal

When we are troubled by a decision, anxious about an exam, or guilty about something we have done or said, it helps if someone lends an ear and offers moral support. "Many of our daily conversations," says a National Institute of Mental Health report, "are actually mutual counseling sessions whereby we exchange the reassurance and advice that help us deal with routine stresses."

When the going really gets rough, such support becomes even more critical. Consider, for example, the testimony of Russian refuseniks, Jews who have been forbidden to emigrate to Israel. Isolated in their communities, with their phones tapped and their mail intercepted, they live in constant danger of arrest. Yet they go on bravely, hoping one day to begin a new life of freedom. What sustains them above all, they attest, is the support of occasional visitors from the American Jewish community. "Only you remain between us and oblivion," said a long-suffering re-fusenik to one such visitor recently. "We survive because we are able to stay in contact with someone who will hear our story."

I know from cruel experience what those words mean. A few years ago, I was the victim of a malevolent colleague, who used our agency's "fraud hot line" to make a false allegation against me. I had, said this still anonymous caller, misused my government position for my own private gain. To make the case stronger, documents had surreptitiously been altered to make it seem as if I had indeed committed a criminal offense.

My superiors, wanting to appear as models of bureaucratic rectitude, gave me no hearing. Instead, they turned the case over to the inspector general of the department I had served loyally for more than two and a half decades. The resulting investigation consumed nearly two years. Agents descended on my office, questioning my subordinates, poring over my files, casting a pall of suspicion over me and my career. I was a marked man, stig-matized, in the words of one official, as "another sleazy civil servant on the take."

I very quickly became an outcast in my own world of work. My psychiatrist-boss turned cool and remote, as if to distance himself from the wrongdoer, and many of my own staff fell away from me. They drifted off together at lunch to exchange the latest gossip, leaving me to lick my wounds. One senior colleague openly exulted over the prospect of taking over my position.

Eventually I was exonerated. But for what seemed an eternity, I lived with crisis and impending doom. No longer did I hurry to the office, looking forward to productive work. Instead, my days were now regularly consumed with the onerous and de-meaning legal tasks required to reassert my character and integ-rity. My self-respect was being shattered.

Looking back at that ordeal, I am convinced that I got through it only because of the unswerving devotion of a loyal friend and that of my family. The seeds of anxiety and depression planted by my stress never took root, never totally overwhelmed me. When the horizon seemed darkest, there was someone around to whom I could reveal my anguish, someone who offered support.

My experience is hardly unique. Researchers have repeatedly demonstrated a vital link between the strength of our social support systems and our emotional and physical resilience under severe stress. They have shown that people in crisis who enjoy contact and support from others—family, friends, or humane professionals in the health-care system—tend not only to maintain higher morale but to suffer fewer physical symptoms and live longer than those who do not.

"Mutual support within a family in times of crisis is critical," says Dr. James J. Strain, psychiatry professor at Mt. Sinai School of Medicine in New York. "Succoring one another, the family never feels alienated or alone. Instead, it feels useful, involved, in control, and able to adapt and reduce stress by pulling together."

Psychologist James Pennebaker recently reported the results of studies of more than 2,000 people who had suffered trauma, including physical abuse, rape, or the death of a loved one. Survivors were healthier, he found, if they managed to confide in someone about the event. Those who hadn't discussed their experiences developed more illness of various sorts—from headaches to lung disease.

In one study, Pennebaker used coroner's records to contact the surviving spouses of men and women who had committed suicide or died in accidents in a large southern city. Those who were open about their grief showed no increase in health problems after their loss. But widows and widowers who kept their anguish to themselves tended to have an abundance of symptoms.

The pain of bereavement seems to leave fewer scars when shared than when it is borne alone.

Pennebaker's research coincides with other accumulating evidence that in unburdening ourselves to another person, we protect ourselves against the potential physical damages of internal stress. Harvard University psychologist David McClelland has shown that people in crisis who tend by nature to keep their innermost feelings to themselves release hormones that lower their immune system's resistance to disease. Reviewing all of the evidence to date, Hebrew University psychiatrist Gerald Caplan concludes that when the stress level is high, people without psychological support suffer as much as ten times the incidence of physical and emotional illness experienced by those who enjoy such support.

It should not surprise us, therefore, that the mortality rate rises sharply for those who need human ties the most and have the fewest. In *The Broken Heart: The Medical Consequences of Loneliness*, James M. Lynch draws startling connections between the absence of companionship and heart disease. People often develop life-threatening heart ailments, he showed, when they find themselves facing life crises without the benefit of human contact. Where there are opportunities for communication, says Lynch, there is less danger of physiological damage. "The rise of human loneliness," he concludes, "may be one of the most serious sources of disease in the 20th century."

Doctors are beginning to recognize that emotional support can be as effective as the most modern technology when it comes to healing. In November 1984, William J. Shroeder underwent surgery for the implantation of an artificial heart. Shroeder's doctors selected him for the experimental operation because they knew he would get strong family support. As they expected, his family was a critical element in the operation's success.

In old age especially, survival appears to depend on whether or not we manage to share our lives with others. Among people over sixty-five, according to the U.S. Bureau of the Census, there are about 1.9 million widowers and 10.8 million widows. The stresses they encounter in adjusting to their loss are reflected in their own subsequent mortality rates. Men, especially, seem to have a difficult time. One study shows that the mortality rate is 61 percent higher for widowers between the ages of fifty-five and sixty-four than for married men in the same age range. Among both men and women who lose their mates, the death rate is higher for those who live alone than for those who share a household with someone else.

Communication has been shown to protect the health of a variety of individuals under stress—from unemployed men to pregnant mothers and aging women. In the poetic words of Carlo Carretto, "We are made by relationships with other people." Even those suffering the most severe trauma appear to be sustained by the communication lifeline. The most extreme example is found among concentration camp survivors now living in both the United States and Israel. As a group, they have an abnormally high incidence of psychiatric problems. A set of symptoms called concentration camp syndrome has afflicted many survivors throughout the decades since the war ended: depression, anxiety, guilt, insomnia, fatigue, constant rumination, chronic irritability, startle reactions, and a host of psychosomatic complaints. A recent study shows, however, that some Holocaust survivors— those who joined clubs offering mutual support and encouragement from others who had undergone the same experience— have been remarkably free of such symptoms. They have been able to work, lead productive lives, and raise healthy children.

Another example of the extraordinary healing power of social supports even for those who have been severely traumatized can be found among combat veterans of the Vietnam War. Many of them, too, have suffered an unusually high rate of psychological problems, including heavy drug abuse and alcoholism. But again, as in the case of concentration camp victims, there are those who emerged from the experience relatively unscathed—without any enduring effects of their war experience. These veterans, it turns out, were fortunate to have returned home to supportive relationships among family and friends. In contrast, many of the Vietnam vets who continue to suffer post-traumatic stress symptoms have enjoyed no such significant contact with others since their return.

Unfortunately, millions of people are without a support system strong enough to meet their needs when facing a crisis. Indeed, far too many among us are without any at all. In our society, the ties that used to bind people together have weakened or disappeared. Once upon a time it was easier for people to find emotional sustenance within the large extended family or the close-knit neighborhood that surrounded them. Now the clan and the circle of neighbors who used to come so quickly to the aid of anyone in trouble have all but vanished. "Communities are brittle and fragile, with a tremendous turnover," says Berkeley sociologist Robert N. Bellah. "There is an element of loneliness not far below the surface."

Newly arrived refugees—1,000,000 in this country in the past decade—are especially vulnerable to the loneliness described by Bellah. "Here you live in an apartment and don't know your neighbors," says Ethiopian immigrant Hailu Fulass. "That's very strange in Ethiopia. When you move in, the neighbors bring you coffee and it's a reception. For someone used to personal contact every day . . . this aloneness creates a sense of emptiness." And back home, he adds, "there are people who interfere with your life, there are people who mind your business . . . but here there is this thing of 'mind your own business.' "

In Vietnam, explains psychotherapist Kim Danh Cook, "You

go to the market once a day. You know everybody; people tell you how to cook the chicken; everybody talks to you. You get very efficient service here, but you don't get the human touch."

This absence of the human touch—this gap in social bonds—is felt by all of us. Recent surveys reveal that it exists in small towns as well as big cities. To fill the gap, many people have sought out one of the many mutual support groups, also called self-help groups, that today offer us the precious opportunity to communicate with others when we are burdened with stress. Such groups, now numbering more than a half million in the United States, are based on the valid belief that when we come together with those who are fighting battles similar to our own, we help ourselves as well as others.

Communication in a Group: The Power of Mutual Support

> Whenever the wind is from the Sea
> Salty and strong
> You are here.
>
> Remembering your zest for hilltops
> And the sturdy surf of your laughter
> Gentles my grief at your going
> And tempers the thought of my own.

That poem, reported by Stanford University psychiatrist Irvin D. Yalom, was written by a woman suffering from breast cancer as a tribute to another victim who had died. Both were members of a mutual support group, one of a number of such groups at Stanford composed of seven to ten women afflicted with the same disease who met weekly for an hour and a half. Each group had two leaders—a psychiatrist or a social worker and a counselor who had also had breast cancer and was now in remission.

Group members opened up their hearts to each other. They shared their fears and desperation not only during meetings but by means of cards and visits when one or another of them was hospitalized. Members helped one another improve communications with surgeons and oncologists, and in smoothing out problematic family relationships. They taught one another what they had learned about life as a result of their encounter with death. And they helped one another face death openly and resolutely, and mourn others in the group who grew sicker or died.

A series of studies in California shows that cancer patients who are members of such support groups fare better than those who do not participate. They suffer fewer mood disturbances, including tension, depression, fatigue, and confusion. Moreover, they make fewer self-defeating attempts to console themselves, such as overeating, smoking, or drinking. And they develop fewer fears and phobias. In general, they are less fatigued and more vigorous in their approach to life—even though they have undergone significant physical deterioration.

Recently, I met with a dozen widows and widowers who gather in the basement of a local church each week. One man told of his experience: "I lost my wife about a half year ago, and for months I needed the wine bottle every night to put me out of it. It got to the point that I was drinking around the clock. I'd sleep two hours, wake two hours, and then sleep a little more. My wife died of a brain tumor, and it was tearing me apart. We were married for thirty-eight years. We had a wonderful marriage—and now nothing. I contemplated suicide. Then I got into this program, and it was the best thing that ever happened to me. Just getting out of the house and having people to talk to saved me." This man's experience has been shared by countless others. Studies have shown that recently bereaved people who are active in such groups experience less anxiety, depression, and physical symptoms, and use fewer tranquilizers and antidepressant drugs.

The group of California breast cancer patients described earlier had mental health professionals as group leaders. The group of widows and widowers I visited did not. Self-help groups are marked by a surprising diversity of approach not only in their use of professional participants and advisers but in such matters as size and the structure and frequency of meetings. None of these things seem to matter—as long as there is human interaction. "The help given does not have the constraints of time, place, or format," points out Frank Riessman, director of the National Self-Help Clearinghouse. "It can be a twenty-four-hour hot line, a buddy on call at any time, immediate concrete assistance as well as emotional help, a three-hour meeting or a five-minute telephone call. It can take place in a basement, an apartment, on a street corner, in a community center, in a church, in an office, on a boat, at a fair, in a rap room in school, in a hospital, in a funeral parlor."

Probably no mutual support group more clearly reflects the healing effects of communication than Alcoholics Anonymous, or A.A. Each chapter is a fellowship of individuals who share their experiences, strengths, and hopes with one another in order to help themselves—and others—recover from the misuse and abuse of alcohol.

The A.A.'s main way of helping people is through the meeting. Usually the most effective type of meeting is the so-called "speaker meeting," in which one or two sober members of the group describe to the others how their alcoholism began, what occurred along the way, and what their lives are like now. An important step for newcomers is to take a "moral inventory," looking realistically at their strengths and then *communicating* their assessments to one another. Newcomers and members are constantly reminded that "we need each other." They are encouraged to call one another at any time of day or night when the urge to drink overtakes them, or when other problems of living seem insurmountable. This communication is the key that unlocks all the other benefits provided by the group experience.

A.A. is only one of a fast-proliferating array of self-help groups now available, to which some fifteen million Americans belong. These groups help people through the entire gamut of life crises. They include, for example, groups in which the jobless organize to help one another find work; burned-out professionals sustain one another; parents of young children with cancer see one another through their ordeal; and widows and widowers attempt to pick up the pieces of their lives. There are groups for couples who are infertile, parents whose child uses drugs, divorced persons, isolated older people, the handicapped, suicide-prone individuals, and former mental patients. (Detailed information about all such groups now in operation across the country is available from the National Self-Help Clearinghouse, 33 West 42nd Street, New York, N.Y. 10036.)

The reasons for joining a group are as varied as the range of tragedies that beset us. Each member's participation in the group, however, increases the chances that one suffering victim will help heal another.

How Communication Heals

"Words are medicine that make us whole and keep us whole." So wrote Harry and Bonaro Overstreet more than thirty years ago. Many of us have assumed that people who are suffering generally seek out psychologists and psychiatrists to talk to for support. This, according to the best evidence, is a myth.

"For the most part," writes University of Rochester psychologist Emory Cowan, "people do *not* bring their personal troubles to mental health professionals." Some do not have the money to pay for costly services. For others, services are not conveniently located. And for still others, such services, as presently packaged, are either unappealing or unacceptable.

Many people prefer to talk to members of the clergy, lawyers, physicians, educators, nurses, hospice workers, welfare and enforcement agents. Others, Cowan writes, seek out "natural caregivers not trained in any professional discipline: neighborhood folks and those whose jobs put them in daily contact with personal troubles."

Why is it that we find such informal communication with others helpful at times of distress? Answers can be gleaned by closely observing what goes on in mutual help groups. Three factors stand out.

To begin with, it is a healing experience simply to put our feelings into words. In his book, *The Theory and Practice of Psychotherapy,* Yalom reports that participants in mutual help groups most value the simple act of "getting things off my chest." It is communication that removes us from what the shipwrecked Robinson Crusoe described as his "island of despair."

Too often, we are reluctant to voice our inner fears and insecurities to others. We fear that if we open up, we will be seen as weak and unworthy. Moreover, we sense that there is a limit to the willingness of others to listen to our tales of woe. We become convinced, as the essayist Montaigne put it, that "I should not betray the story of my life." The experiences of people in mutual support groups suggest otherwise. They find that expressing even their most morbid concerns helps them to build a bond with others who are equally troubled. There is nothing that cannot be discussed and understood by the members of the group.

In our daily lives as well, we need not search terribly hard to find fellow sufferers. It is often surprising how, when we unburden ourselves to even casual friends, we discover that they have had their own comparably traumatic experiences. "Anguish and heartbreak may not be distributed evenly throughout the world," writes Harold Kushner, "but they are distributed very widely. Everyone gets his share. If we knew the facts, we would very rarely find someone whose life was to be envied." And sharing our grief with fellow sufferers makes our own burden lighter.

Second, communication helps us to recognize that others who face similar problems manage to survive. In *The Inventor's Suffering*, Honore Balzac wrote: "The first thought of a man, be he a leper or a prisoner, a sinner or an invalid, is to have a companion in his fate." One of the sources of relief most frequently cited by members of mutual help groups, reports Leon H. Levy, is "the discovery through group discussion that one is not unique in having a problem." And this carries with it the hope, says Levy, that a way out must exist. When we communicate with others, we discover models we can follow.

Recently, at a celebration honoring Everett Alvarez on the twentieth anniversary of his capture, his fellow POWs paid him tribute. Said Edward Anthony Davis: "Ev, I used you as a benchmark. About a week or two after I was taken prisoner, someone told me you'd been there a year. I adopted this thought: My God, that man has been there so much longer than I. As long as he is sane, then I can stay sane. If he was still hanging in there, the rest of us could hang in there. If he could make it, we could make it. If he could be strong, we could be strong."

During the months in which I was being subjected to an unjustified investigation, I found surprising strength in my contacts with someone who had experienced—and survived—a similar ordeal. I came to realize from my talks with him that the crisis I faced *could* be endured and conquered.

Third, we learn through communication that our reactions to stress are not unnatural. More than two decades ago, psychologist Stanley Schachter asked college student-volunteers into his laboratory and told them that in a few minutes they would be receiving frightening electrical shocks. But he gave the prospective victims a choice of waiting alone in a comfortable room with some magazines, waiting with others who were not in the experiment, or with those who would also be shocked. The result: Most chose to wait with others who were facing the same trauma.

Why?

Schachter concluded that in upsetting and threatening situations we have a strong need to compare our emotional reactions with those of others. Being unduly anxious, sad, or upset is generally not approved of in our society, and many of us struggling under stress are uncomfortable because we see ourselves as being more upset than we should be—the victims, perhaps, of emotional disturbance. The company of others gives us the assurance that we are really not "going crazy." The old adage that "misery loves company" may be true, in other words, because we want to see ourselves as no sadder or more upset than others in similar circumstances.

Writer-producer Barbara Gordon, who rebuilt her life after a mental breakdown, wrote a book about her experience. In the years that followed, she says, she received letters and phone calls from thousands of people who had faced the terror of starting over, sometimes alone, sometimes with only a fraction of what had once been a family. "Their stories amazed me," writes Gordon. "Trying to begin life over did not make me a freak. No, I was not the only person who felt she was re-creating herself out of whole cloth. . . . They too had floundered in passivity, been paralyzed by fears of stigma, immobilized by loneliness."

When he lost his wife of fifty-two years, Kurt Fox was sure he had reached the end of the road. "I was mad at God," he says. "There I was in a suddenly empty house. I literally thought

I was losing my mind." Then he joined a group known as the Widowed Persons Service, which provides counsel, support, and assistance to newly widowed persons. "Perhaps the biggest thing is to be able to talk to someone who's been through it," he says. "I found that it's important for a person to hear that in spite of their craziest fantasies while they're bereaved, they're normal."

Only by communicating with others can we learn that our own distress in the face of crisis is actually universal. The Foundation for Sudden Infant Death was organized more than twenty years ago by a Connecticut couple whose baby had succumbed to crib death, which is still a mysterious tragedy. In the local groups of this organization, parents can come to recognize that the grief and guilt they feel are no different from that experienced by others in the same situation. "Whenever I can't seem to function," said one mother, "I call someone in the foundation. 'Am I nuts? Am I going crazy?' It's comforting to hear her say, 'No, I've been through this, too. It's part of the natural grieving process.'"

But there is yet another precious benefit to be derived from communicating when we are beset by stress. In choosing to interact with others rather than withdrawing into ourselves, we are demonstrating a willingness to do something about our suffering—to control our fate. And it is this sense of personal control that turns out to be one of the most important characteristics of those who, in the end, prevail over life's adversities.

Though my wing is closely bound,
My heart's at liberty;
Prison walls cannot control
The flight, the freedom of the soul.
JEANNE GUYON
The Prisoner's Song

2.
Control: Taking Charge of Your Life

A few years ago, my father and two brothers died within a span of eighteen months. I watched helplessly as the ravages of age depleted my father's body and mind. At the same time, my brothers were succumbing to the savagery of cancer— their bodies wasted, their capacity for pleasure ended, their terror and pain unyielding. And then one day these vital realities of my life were gone. Bereavement times three.

I felt desolated. With so much of my past wiped away, the future seemed empty and worthless. My natural optimism, my instinct for taking charge and bending each day to my will, suddenly vanished. The world was spinning out of orbit, and it seemed to me that nothing I might do could ever set it right.

Most of us who have faced devastating life crises have shared that feeling. Whether we emerge from these experiences victorious or defeated depends largely on whether we manage to regain some mastery over our existence. One important way to do so is to reestablish the rhythm of life that is so often destroyed by traumatic events.

Order Out of Chaos: Creating a Routine

"Order," wrote Alexander Pope, "is heaven's first law." The emergence of order out of chaos, of dependability out of uncertainty, are the consoling images offered us by prophets and poets throughout the centuries. We know today that such images are not merely fancies conjured up to provide comfort in the face of the unknown. Science offers persuasive evidence that an invisible order indeed underlies the world about us—and our inner world as well.

Each day, as the earth turns on its axis, we experience the familiar rhythm of light and darkness. The moon's revolution, too, pulls our atmosphere into a cycle of predictable change. Night follows day, seasons alter, the tides ebb and flow. In concert with the turning earth, animals and plants also live by an orderly rhythm. Mollusks and fish, cats and baboons, marigolds and humans—indeed most living organisms—show a daily cycle of activity and rest. Time-lapse photography has captured the rhythms of plant life, showing how leaves lift and drop, open and close every twenty-four hours.

Though we may be unaware of it, an orderly ebb and flow also marks our own daily existence. Body temperature, blood pressure, pulse, respiration, are constantly changing to the rhythm of a reliable refrain. So, too, are the levels of essential hormones in the blood and of biochemicals throughout the nervous system. Laboratory studies have now disclosed an inexorable regularity in almost every physiological function, from the deposit of fat or sugar in the liver to the rate at which our cells divide.

The life of each of us is fastened to the celestial and biological order. Interrupt the rhythm of the planets and you invite apocalyptic disaster; alter the regular tempo of the heartbeat and cardiovascular catastrophe is sure to follow; disturb the orderly life of cells and malignant tumors grow. Even a disruption in the sleep and rest cycle—or of the regular rhythm of nightly dreaming—can pose a threat to our well-being.

It is easy enough to recognize the importance of a reliable physical universe to our survival, but we are less likely to acknowledge a craving for orderliness in our psychological environment. Yet it is embedded in all of us. The yearning for a sense of order and routine in life begins early in childhood, and when it remains unrequited there is anxiety, anger, and despair. As young children grow, they display this need for an orderly existence in their insatiable delight with the repetitive and familiar—the songs and rhymes that accompany feeding, the endless peekaboo games, and the rituals of bedtime.

Throughout our adult lives, our emotional well-being also depends on recurrent and dependable themes, familiar motifs that give our existence a comforting coherence. When the ordinary routines of everyday life—eating, working, sleeping, waking—are interrupted by travel or by a move, many people feel bereft and at a loss. Each day seems disconnected from those that came yesterday and that will follow tomorrow. "I should be as happy as I can be," a young mother said to me recently after moving into a lovely new community. "But I'm depressed. I miss all the things I used to take for granted—that I depended on so much without actually knowing it."

It is just this comforting sense of orderliness and regularity that is demolished by traumatic events. Life suddenly takes on a rudderless quality. Lost is what Samuel Clark called "the eternal fitness of things." The bedrocks of our existence turn to quicksand. Nothing can be anticipated with certainty.

"I've lost my hold on life," a recently widowed neighbor complained to me. "All the rhythm of my existence is gone." After their ordeal, crime victims frequently complain that "the world is suddenly out of whack," and "things no longer work the way they used to." They can no longer see the world as a safe place.

At such times, it is critical to reestablish some order and routine in our existence, even if it is only in a corner of daily life. That is what I did, for example, when my own threefold grief devastated me. I had begun to find that even the simple act of getting up in the morning to face the day seemed impossible. Life had become, as Henry James wrote in describing his own to Edith Wharton, "a nightmare from which there is no waking save by sleep." I deliberately decided, therefore, to get up each dawn and sit at my typewriter as I have done for decades. Although the pages I produced were few and inadequate, I knew when I arose from my desk each day that I had stayed in control of myself as a writer.

Senator Jacob Javits is the victim of amyotrophic lateral sclerosis (ALS), also known as Lou Gehrig's disease, an incurable neurological disorder. He is restricted to a wheelchair. His muscles are weak, and he must wear a collar to hold up his head. A portable respirator helps him catch his breath. "But as long as your brain can function," he insists, "you can make a contribution."

Javits has described his typical daily routine. "I get up at seven. It takes a couple hours for the nurse to give me the necessary assistance in the morning. I have a light breakfast, and then I'm pushed down in a wheelchair to my office. I go in as many times a week as I can." The routine, he is convinced, gives his life a coherence in the face of chaos.

Ambassador Bruce L. Laingen recalls that he made sure he shaved every day during his fourteen months as a hostage in Iran, something he does not even do at home. "That daily practice was critical," Laingen told me recently. "It helped preserve my fading self-image."

In the Nazi concentration camps, many devout Jews kept their sanity by maintaining an unflinching attachment to the rituals of their faith. They secretly occupied themselves in attempts to prepare the rudiments of the Passover seder feast, or in painstakingly crafting willow branches used for centuries in celebrating the Hebrew thanksgiving festival known as Succot. In the museum that now occupies the bloody ground of Auschwitz, a visitor can find remnants of prayer books, Torah scrolls, prayer shawls, skullcaps, and other religious objects that lent some structure even to the pathetic lives of those swallowed up in the Holocaust.

Many inmates of the Nazi camps even sought rulings on religious matters from the surviving rabbis in their midst, as though they were still functioning freely in a normal community. "Questions on fine points of Jewish law," writes Holocaust historian Irving J. Rosenbaum, "were directed to a scholarly rabbi, and answers were offered. Dedication to the law was expressed not in the abstract, but in the minutiae of daily life even *in extremis*. Thus, a semblance of normality was restored to the inmates of the vicious madhouses. . . ."

The fact that the rituals with which these survivors occupied themselves were religious in content was, I believe, incidental to their ultimate psychological value. What counted most was that they sounded familiar and recurring themes even in the shadow of the crematorium.

One POW returning from six years of captivity in Vietnam

described to me quite a different sort of daily routine that, he believes, saved him from being crushed by his ordeal. After a few months of solitude, he realized that his daydreams—of freedom, family, sex, work—had become his main source of emotional support. But soon enough, they began to wear thin. They intruded throughout the day—while he was reading, eating, trying to sleep, or sitting in the latrine. As a result, they were beginning to lose their value as a means of escape.

"I finally figured out that what I really needed to survive was to control those fantasies, to organize them as a special daily event," he says. "So I decided to reserve a couple hours every afternoon for the experience. After lunch, while lying in my cell, I would run a particular movie of my life. One day I would see my kids off to school and go through a whole day with them. Another day I would make love to my wife. I savored every detail—the hints of anticipation in our telephone conversations, all the delicious hours in bed together, even the small talk at breakfast the next morning. On another day I would teach a class of Navy recruits, going through an entire lecture. At times I would become irritated with an arrogant student, at other times I would regale the class with jokes. The important thing was that I was no longer squandering my fantasies promiscuously in fragments throughout the day and night. I had a special time reserved for them. I had something to look forward to—and the routine helped organize my empty life and keep me afloat." If only in his own mind, this lonely captive had established some control over his empty world. And he survived.

Without a sense of control, we become vulnerable to a feeling of impotence—a conviction that we are altogether helpless in shaping our destiny. Exactly how that happens—and what we can do to prevent it—is now clear both from experiments in psychological laboratories and from experiences in real life.

How You Learn
to Feel Helpless

The dog, strapped into a harness, receives a series of electrical shocks, each lasting five seconds, delivered at random intervals. There is no way it can avoid the shocks or escape from them before the five seconds are up.

The next day the dog is placed in a so-called hurdle box that allows it to jump to safety. From time to time the light inside the box is dimmed, and a few seconds later a shock is administered through the floor of the compartment. Now the animal can avoid the shock altogether by jumping over the hurdle into the adjoining compartment when the warning light is dimmed, or it can jump after the electricity is turned on. If the dog stays where it is, the shock continues for a full fifty seconds.

The results of this classic experiment were dramatic. All of the dogs used in the experiment had unlimited opportunities to learn to avoid the shock or to escape it—but they did not. Their experiences of the day before led them to make no attempt to leap over the hurdle. They simply accepted the shock for the full fifty seconds.

Why did the experimental animals lapse into passive acceptance of pain? The researchers—University of Pennsylvania psychologist Martin E. P. Seligman and his colleagues—called it learned helplessness. While strapped in the harness, the dogs "concluded" that nothing they could do would have any effect on whether they received a shock or for how long. When they moved to the hurdle box, they had no incentive to try to escape.

In similar experiments, this weakening of efforts to respond at all in the face of harsh events has been found in a variety of species—monkeys, cats, mice, birds, fish—and, most important, in humans. In one study, for example, college students were subjected to an earsplitting noise. They were told they could stop the noise by learning how to manipulate some control devices, but actually these devices had no effect. Later, when placed in a situation where it would have been easy to turn off the noise, the students made no effort and simply put up with it until the experimenter called a halt.

In real life, we learn to feel helpless in exactly the same way. Inevitably we encounter brutal shocks and "noises" that we can do nothing about—misfortunes such as bereavement, sudden accidents or crimes, life-threatening illnesses, or broken relationships. The tendency at such times is to yield all sense of dominion over our fate, and to develop a debilitating psychological condition best described as "give-up-itis."

If we are to survive life's darkest hours, we must wrest back control of our lives when it suddenly slips out of our grasp.

Seizing the Initiative

Try to imagine yourself as a captive. The activities you take for granted are no longer under your control. You cannot eat when you are hungry, enjoy a walk or a nap when you feel like it, or even urinate or defecate when nature calls. Your entire life has slipped out of your grasp.

Most of the POWs I've talked with say that the realization they had lost command over their existence was the really awful thing about their ordeal. Losing control over their daily lives was more critical than their more exotic and widely publicized sufferings—the threats of execution, hunger, beatings, torture, and isolation. After he returned from Iran, one hostage described what was for him the essence of life—"the simple act of brushing my teeth when I get up in the morning, just because I feel like it."

Those captives who triumphed over their adversity have a lesson to teach us all: They managed somehow to reassert a degree of command over their destiny. Instead of becoming totally passive and helpless, they fastened on every opportunity they could find to reaffirm their lost power.

Whenever hostage John Limbert's Iranian guards came into his room, he invited them to sit down. "They became *my* guests," says Limbert, "and in this small way, I established command of the situation. I created the unmistakable sense that this was *my* space, *my* territory, and it did wonders for my well-being."

Early in 1980, when an Algerian delegation made a ceremonial visit, Limbert and a few friends had some candies and fruits left over from their Christmas service. "We made a little plate filled with these goodies," recalls Limbert, "and as the Algerians sat down, we offered the refreshments to them and to the Iranian cameraman who was there to film the occasion for propaganda purposes. The message got through. *We* were the gracious hosts, and *they* were our guests. They were visiting at our pleasure, not the other way around."

Michael Metrinko, held in solitary confinement for more than four months in Iran, gave up his three-pack-a-day cigarette habit. The reason: Metrinko had given up the habit in the past, and he knew that he would probably turn angry and abrasive as a result. "I was offered cigarettes, but I turned them down," Metrinko explained to me, "because I wanted to make sure that I stayed irritable enough to control the relationship between me and my captors." He felt he needed that aggressive edge to prevent his guards from getting the upper hand. "I wanted to make absolutely sure that my reservoir of resentment was never exhausted."

Metrinko was able to show his student guards that he could still control events. "I refused to accept their special holiday food because I wanted them to know that it was just propaganda—a total sham," he recalls. "I even turned down an offer for the company of other hostages. I had worked out a routine of exercise and reading in solitary, and I was not about to yield control of my life space."

In February 1986, Soviet dissident Anatoly B. Shcharansky was released after nine years in Soviet prison and labor camps. On the day he was freed, he flung himself in the snow and refused to continue on his way because his escorts tried to confiscate a book of Psalms that his wife had sent him from Israel. "I said I would not leave the country without the Psalms, which helped me so much," Shcharansky reported later. "I lay down in the snow and said, 'Not another step.' " Then, when he was told to walk off the plane that had brought him to West Berlin and freedom, he did so—but he walked in a zigzag. Shcharansky wanted to assert his control until the final climactic seconds of his captivity.

Embedded in these episodes are hints of the take-charge attitude we all need to help us survive when a crisis threatens to overwhelm us. Psychiatrist Michael Rutter points to such an approach as the key in handling the stresses in his own life. "It seems to me that the turning points come when I resolve to do something about them. I am very struck by the fact that what is reparative is not necessarily succeeding in remedying the crisis, but in taking steps to do so. There is often a long delay before you know whether what you have done has had any benefit. But you feel better long before you know that. What you need is to *act* on your troubles."

At the University of Chicago, researcher-psychologists Suzanne C. Kobasa and Salvatore R. Maddi have identified a sense of control as an important element in what they describe as "hardiness." They find that people who resist stress, who do not succumb to crises by becoming ill, operate with the belief that they can exert control over events.

In one study, Kobasa and Maddi analyzed the incidence of life stresses among hundreds of business executives. Those who stayed healthy in the face of crises felt that they had what it takes to exert a tangible impact on their surroundings. On a questionnaire, for example, they categorically disagreed with such statements as "No matter how hard you work, you never really seem to reach your goals," or "This world is run by a few people in power, and there's not much a person can do about it."

The act of exerting control, laboratory research now shows, actually changes our body chemistry in ways that allow us to stave off both physical disease and depression. The evidence stems from studies of both animals and humans.

Rats that are able to press a lever in order to avoid a shock incur less physiological damage—for example, weight loss and gastric lesions—than rats that receive the same amount of shock but are physically restrained and therefore cannot respond. The rats that are allowed to control the "crisis" maintain lower blood levels of cortisol, a hormone secreted by the pituitary gland under stress or during emotional upset and found in excess among people suffering from depression. Studies of other animals show the same thing. One team found, for example, that rhesus monkeys able to exert control over a disturbing noise showed cortisol levels similar to animals that were not exposed to the noise at all—and the levels in both groups were significantly lower than those of monkeys that had no influence on the situation.

The results hold up with humans as well. In one study, subjects were asked to perform mental arithmetic tasks while listening to noise. Some of them were offered a choice between intensities; they could exert control. A comparison group were subjected to the same noise levels but had no say in the matter.

The group that felt that they were controlling events showed less discomfort and secreted less cortisol.

The pattern appears to persist throughout our lives. Harvard developmental psychologist Jerome Kagan has found that babies are less anxious in the presence of strangers when they have some control over the environment. For example, when they can influence the scenario of play with a stranger, or direct the action of the toys surrounding them, their distress is muted.

At the other end of the life span, Yale psychologist Judith Rodin studied everyone over sixty-two who entered one of two major hospitals in the New Haven vicinity. "We selected at random from a group scheduled to enter a nursing home on discharge from the hospital and gave half of them an opportunity to participate in the decision," Rodin reports. "Initially, both groups had similar health status. After one year, those in the group given some control over the decision to enter a nursing home were healthier, and fewer had died than in the group given no choice."

For those already in nursing homes, Rodin was struck by the impact of such seemingly trivial changes as allowing them to decide when to go to a movie, or how to arrange their rooms. As a result of such choices, their health and emotional well-being improved, and the death rate dropped.

"The changes seem trivial to people with a broad range of choices," says Rodin. "But against the backdrop of no choice at all, having any choice is dramatic." She believes that by providing options, she changed the aged individuals' approach to life. "The residents had a greater sense of efficacy," explains Rodin, "so they responded to others differently, and that enabled their families and nurses to respond to them more positively." At the core of their well-being was a self-perception all of us need during times of misfortune—that we are still the manager of life's journey, no matter how rough the road.

Staying in Command in the Face of Illness

Nancy Wechsler, a psychologist, faces the possibility that she will become physically and mentally helpless by middle age. Twenty years ago her father, psychoanalyst Milton Wechsler, called her home from college to tell her that her mother had developed the devastating neurological disorder known as Huntington's chorea. The disease is transmitted genetically, so there was a fifty-fifty chance that Nancy would also develop it. If she did, she would suffer some of the most gruesome symptoms in medical annals—tics and tremors, grotesque clumsiness, flailing limbs, and drunken gait. She would deteriorate psychologically as well—first with growing irritability and forgetfulness, then with an intellectual collapse so severe that she might easily be mistaken for someone with severe schizophrenia.

In the face of such a threat, one option for Nancy was to back off from what might lie ahead. But that's not what she did. Instead she confronted her crisis head-on—by beginning research on victims of Huntington's. "Part of the reason for my own doctoral dissertation," she says, "was to help me sort out and clarify my own feelings by going through the process of talking to people in my shoes." Nancy has published numerous articles about the fears and psychological defenses of those at risk for Huntington's, and how counselors can go about supporting them.

Nancy faces the threat rather than the reality of illness. But her response demonstrates how important it is to stay in command when we actually do fall ill. For when our bodies falter, we are especially vulnerable to losing control.

The last sixteen years of Sigmund Freud's life were filled with terrible suffering. Growths on his cheek and palate had been diagnosed as cancerous, and thirty-one operations were in store

43

to keep the disease under control. Freud's mouth was permanently contracted, and part of his tongue had to be removed. A large prosthesis—a type of giant denture intended to shut off his upper mouth from his nasal cavity—caused Freud unrelenting pain and misery, so much so that he nicknamed it "the monster." As described by Leon Prochnik:

> For Freud, who had always taken great pleasure in food, eating was now an agony, and from here on, he would rarely take his meals in the presence of others. In talking he frequently held the prosthesis in place with his thumb. For the remainder of his days, Freud's speech would be defective—nasal and thick, its quality similar to that produced by a cleft palate. His hearing, also impaired by the operation, would soon leave him totally deaf on his right side—his "listening" side—so that the position of his chair and his famed analyst's couch had to be reversed.

Nevertheless, in spite of all this suffering, Freud stayed in command of his life and work. "I have never realized," he wrote, "that the older one grows, the more there is to do. . . ." Like the rest of us, he experienced some self-doubt. At one point, after yet another painful operation, he cried out, "I can't go on any longer!" But he did go on, continuing to write and to see patients—and to refuse all drugs that might have alleviated his suffering. "I prefer to think in torment," he insisted, "than not to be able to think clearly."

Freud wanted to stay in control—and he did. In his last years, he originated and developed a number of his most renowned theories of human behavior. He produced a torrent of scientific papers, constantly organized international conferences, and kept up a ceaseless correspondence with other analysts around the world.

Unfortunately, for many of us the potential for staying in control in the face of illness is often reduced because of the way we are treated as patients. In the office of a modern doctor or in a hospital room, we are likely to experience, in the words of physician Lawrence K. Altman, "a kind of humiliation that seems to grow out of vulnerability, nakedness, of being handled, left exposed to be clinically peered at and examined like grapefruit in a grocery." We are made to feel powerless, totally unable to affect events around us.

We don't have to be. Even cancer patients, who often feel totally powerless in dealing with their physicians, have learned in therapy groups to improve their relationship with their doctors. They rehearsed new methods of asserting themselves, requesting more time from their doctors and demanding information about their illness. Some learned to ask to see their medical charts or to inspect their X rays, and others assumed responsibility by refusing further medication when that decision seemed sound.

Our POWs in Vietnam demonstrated to a remarkable degree the astounding capacity we all have to manage our own physical well-being. The North Vietnamese captors offered them no dental treatment, so the POWs developed their own brand of self-help dentistry. They used sterilized sharpened nails, fishbones, razors, and other such instruments in a "home" treatment program. When salt was available they hoarded it to treat infections. Some men even developed self-hypnosis techniques to help them through their discomfort.

Every six months, the captors provided the POWs with a tube labeled "antiseptic toothpaste" in English. The POWs used it in surprisingly imaginative ways. They placed the toothpaste not only on painful teeth but on burns. They used it as an antacid, as a lotion to prevent rectal itching caused by hemorrhoids and pinworm infestations, to clean wounds, and to control infections resulting from insect bites.

45

In the view of psychologist John E. Deaton, the POWs gained strength "by devoting their efforts to controlling, changing, or mastering the environment." Such tactics helped to ensure not only their physical survival but their psychological survival as well. When stress is overwhelming, it is critical to keep proving to yourself that you still are, in the poet's words, the master of your fate, the captain of your soul.

Controlling Life by an Eyebrow

David Rabin, forty-nine, is a professor of medicine at Vanderbilt University. Like Senator Javits, he has ALS, or Lou Gehrig's disease. There is no treatment or cure for the disease, which causes gradual paralysis throughout the body and premature death.

"Among the catalog of terrifying diseases one learns at medical school," Rabin recalls, "none frightened me more than amyotrophic lateral sclerosis." He remembers being introduced in class to his first patient with the disease, a man imprisoned in a wheelchair, "so small, so emaciated, so vulnerable, so insignificant." Rabin can still hear the booming voice of the neurologist as he rendered the prognosis: " 'Hopeless! This is creeping paralysis! He will be demeaned, isolated, frustrated, unable to communicate, and probably will be dead in six months.' "

The same disease has already reduced Rabin to a shell of his former self. "The course that the illness followed was straight out of a textbook," writes his psychiatrist wife, Pauline I. Rabin. First there was stiffness of the legs, then weakness. Soon the disease caused paralysis of the lower limbs. Weakness of the hands gave way to total wasting of small muscles and loss of function of upper limbs. As the paralysis extended, David became a quadriplegic. Next the tongue lost its function, and he could form words and swallow only with the greatest difficulty.

Rabin, who pursued an active and successful academic career, was forty-five when ALS was diagnosed. Determined to continue to live and work as normally as possible, he adapted to the physical limitations imposed by the illness. When he could no longer examine patients, he served as a consultant. When he could no longer get to the hospital, he had the laboratory teams come to his home for regular conferences. In this way, he was able to direct an active research program.

When Rabin's hands could no longer turn the pages of books, he got a machine that turned the pages automatically. And when he lost his voice altogether, he found a computer as a vehicle for speaking and writing. Here is Rabin's amazing electronic communication odyssey, described in his own words:

> . . . I lost the use of my hands more than two years ago, and as I faced a tracheotomy, my worst nightmare was whether this would finally turn me into a nonperson—every sensory perception intact but strictly one-way traffic.
>
> Fortunately, miraculously, none of this would prove correct. On the day after my tracheotomy, I received a letter from a fellow physician who also has ALS telling me . . . that a computer was available that could be operated with a single switch. . . . The significance of the single switch is that it can be operated by anyone, however physically handicapped, who retains the function of one muscle group. For me, my eyebrow muscle is strong enough to depress a very light switch and thereby gives me access to the full power of the computer.
>
> The screen presents the alphabet to me. A pointer ("cursor") moves at a speed that I select, and I press the switch when the pointer is next to the letter I want. This opens an electronic dictionary to a page of words beginning with the desired letter.

The process is repeated, and with the aid of the pointer, a word is selected. It takes longer to explain than to do!

In conjunction with a printer and voice synthesizer, the eyebrow-driven computer has revolutionized Rabin's life.

> I talk to my family—that is most wonderful. I can make conversation with friends—the jokes take a little longer, but they don't seem to mind. I can work independently again— write papers, review manuscripts, cooperate by mail with other scientists—and I am able to interact with the persons in my laboratory. I write out my ideas before we meet and we sum up afterward. Because of the loyalty and devotion of this group— and for me the indispensable ability to communicate—our research continues to be original and productive.

During the past three years, Rabin's group has pioneered research in male contraception and has made important contributions to the understanding of various processes of body metabolism. In August 1982, his comprehensive textbook on endocrinology and metabolism was published. Recently he received a prestigious award from his university for working "toward ways to be constructive in the midst of a destructive disease."

Rabin's history, dramatic as it is, is not unique. When pushed to the limit, many have demonstrated a similar invincibility of spirit. They have proclaimed by their actions that control of life is still possible—even against seemingly impossible odds.

Changing the World for Others

On March 15, 1982, actress Theresa Saldana was repeatedly stabbed on a Los Angeles street near her home. Her life was saved, but she discovered soon enough that the aftermath of such a nightmare can be even worse. Hers was a classic case of post-traumatic stress. For months she felt lost. She relived the attack in all its horror in her dreams. She was reduced to a helpless, nagging dependence on her mother and father. Her marriage faltered, partly because, like many victims, she was convinced that no one—not even her husband—could really understand her terror and anguish. And she felt stigmatized by the scars left on her body by the attacker.

During the months of her painful recovery, Saldana found herself in touch with others in similar straits, and she became convinced that they needed an organization to provide the kind of emotional support doctors and nurses are unable to give. "Nobody can understand what it feels like to be attacked by another human being," she said.

To fill the void, Saldana eventually founded a group called Victims for Victims. Working with the district attorney's office, her goal was simply "to provide support, advice, companionship, and help to anyone who's interested."

"Everyone in this room tonight is here for the same reason," she said to the large crowd that turned out at her first meeting, "because it's so hard to get through something like this, and because for so long, nobody—not even our families or our closest friends—could understand how horrible we felt. At times we were afraid of people. We even hated people, and we felt like the worst thing in the world had happened to us. And I think everyone in this room would agree that it was completely natural to feel that way. So we're together now. We understand each other, we can really talk to each other, and we can help each other. And we can help not only those who are in this room tonight but everybody out there who is or may become a victim."

Many people struck by tragedy find that the road back opens only if they work, as Theresa did, to control and change the forces that brought them low. Here, for example, are three cases of grieving mothers described by writer Fred Ferretti:

- Odile Stern's eighteen-year-old daughter, Michele, was kidnapped, raped, and shot to death in Atlanta, where she was attending college. A year later, Mrs. Stern helped found the organization known as Parents of Murdered Children of New York State.

- The life of Candy Lightner's thirteen-year-old daughter, Cari, ended instantly when she was hit by a drunken driver in Fair Oaks, California. Mrs. Lightner emerged from her grief to form MADD—Mothers Against Drunken Drivers—a self-help group comprised of mothers whose children have been similarly slaughtered. MADD now has 450 chapters in 47 states and a mailing list of 600,000 people. As this book was being written, the man who killed Cari Lightner injured still another girl. "This doesn't set me back," said Mrs. Lightner. "It makes me angry and makes me want to go forward even more."

- Eileen Stevens's twenty-year-old son, Chuck, died after a fraternity hazing incident at Alfred University in upstate New York. He was locked in a car trunk and instructed to drink bottles of beer, whiskey, and wine. Later, when the trunk was opened, Chuck was found unconscious. A victim of acute alcohol poisoning, he never woke up. Mrs. Stevens, observing that "tragedy has a way of getting priorities in order," founded CHUCK, Committee to Halt Useless College Killings.

In each of these cases, the bereaved mother could not prevent the tragic events. But for each, the road to healing was paved with the energy that comes from helping to shape events through advocacy and political action. National Self-Help Clearinghouse director Frank Riessman is convinced that a major benefit of mutual help groups is that they offer the victim a sense of "empowerment." When people join together with others to deal with common problems, they are exercising control over some aspect of their lives. The result is an increase in motivation that cannot easily be imposed from the outside. In successful therapy groups for women with breast cancer, for example, many patients begin to speak out for the rights of cancer patients, and they campaign for political issues affecting them—including fairer tax regulations to cover the cost of breast prostheses and other extraordinary expenses brought about by their illness.

After Michele's death, Mrs. Stern became active in the Victims Services Agency, which offered Families of Homicide Victims as a mutual support group. After a year of simply sharing pain and anger, she was convinced that the group had to go further. "Self-help is not enough," she says. So she helped form a committee to assist in counseling parents of homicide victims on how to deal with the criminal justice system—how, for example, to make sure that their grief and outrage are heard by those responsible for bringing the criminals to justice. Today legislation is under way in New York State that will ensure counseling for parents of missing children. Mrs. Stern, who is also active in the gun control movement, constantly encourages her fellow victims to go beyond self-help to advocacy. "Now," she says, "I feel Michele's death has not been in vain."

Mrs. Lightner describes herself as an advocate and activist. She has picketed the California governor's office as well as the White House, and she was appointed to a Presidential Blue Ribbon Commission on Drunk Driving. As soon as the MADD organization became public, people flocked to join. Today the group is concerned not only with offering mutual support for survivors but also with legislation to stiffen the penalties for drunk driving and other legal and social changes. Members of the various chapters send out pamphlets describing the rights of survivors, and each chapter has an assistance program for them.

The work gives participants a healing sense of *doing* something about their irretrievable losses.

Mrs. Stevens is a beneficiary of that healing. She speaks and writes to hundreds of fraternities across the country, and she has helped seventeen states pass laws that will control the kind of hazing activities that ended her son's life. "I travel, I speak, I share information. That's a very big part of my life," she says. "I've channeled my grief in a positive direction." Her goal is to make certain that other children will not be destroyed, and that other mothers will not have to endure her suffering.

The efforts of these women underscore an important lesson: Working to effect change gives purpose to life when its very meaning seems to have vanished forever.

If we have our own *why* of life,
we shall get along with almost any *how*.
FRIEDRICH WILHELM NIETZSCHE
Twilight of the Idols

3.
Conviction: Giving Purpose to Your Pain

When Marcia awoke before dawn one morning last winter, she reached across the bed to touch Robert, her husband of twenty years. She felt only the cold blanket and pillow—and the silence told her she was alone. She quickly turned on the light and confirmed her terror. It was only 4:00 A.M., and the house was empty. In an instant, she was at the window to check the car. Gone. On the snow-covered driveway below, fresh tire tracks glistened in the moonlight.

Two hours later, a police officer told Marcia how her husband died. He had driven down the nearby highway at screaming speed, veered onto a narrow road, then aimed his car over an embankment and into the river.

Robert ended his life because, as he had recently told Marcia, "everything I've worked for—everything that means anything to me—is turned to ashes." The business that had been his all-consuming passion for more than a dozen years was failing, and Robert confronted a void. "There's no aim left in life," he said after dinner the night before he died. "Nothing makes sense anymore."

Robert's suicide shows the devastation that can follow when life seems suddenly without meaning. It underscores how vital it is to grasp an anchoring purpose for our existence in the face of crushing stress. Viennese psychiatrist Viktor Frankl learned this lesson as a survivor of the Nazis' Auschwitz and Dachau death camps. The person who no longer had a goal, he observed, was unlikely to survive. The search for meaning, Frankl concluded, is "the primary force in life."

Meaninglessness: The Unrecognized Neurosis

Today's practicing psychiatrists and psychologists pay surprisingly little attention to our need to find threads of meaning in the sometimes tattered fabric of human existence. Instead, many mental health professionals search for the roots of misery in their patients' frustrated power needs, aggressive impulses, or sexual longings.

A look at the American Psychiatric Association's official Diagnostic and Statistical Manual of Mental Disorders is revealing. This is the authoritative A to Z list of what can go wrong with your mental health. It describes in exquisite detail more than 230 emotional and mental afflictions. But you will search in vain for any mention of "meaninglessness" as a psychological disease or even a symptom.

Yet countless individuals beset by anxiety and depression report that their basic problem is an existence that is without meaning. Studies show that people seeking psychotherapy, when asked why, often give as reasons "purposelessness" or "drifting without a goal" or "a need for meaningfulness in my life," more frequently than "to change how I relate to people" or "loneliness." Frankl believes that the symptoms of more than 20 percent of America's psychiatric patients are spawned by living in a universe that is, for them, without meaning. Psychoanalyst Carl Jung, were he alive, would not be surprised. "About a third of my cases," he wrote, "are not suffering from any clinically definable neurosis, but from the senselessness and aimlessness of their lives." Said Jung: "Meaning makes a great many things endurable—perhaps everything."

When we suffer pain and trauma, the danger of losing a sense of meaning and a guiding purpose in life is especially profound. When, for example, a loved one dies, a child goes astray, or a career is jeopardized, it is natural to conclude that our suffering is without rhyme or reason. The novelist Albert Camus recognized how devastating the result can be. "I have seen many people die because life for them was not worth living," he wrote. "From this I conclude that the question of life's meaning is the most urgent question of all."

Camus's observation is borne out by studies of suicide notes. Few of the messages, report suicide experts Edwin S. Shneidman and Norman L. Farberow, are concerned primarily with failing health, rejection, or finances. Instead, they speak of being "tired of life," of suicide as "a way out," or of there being "no point in living."

Three centuries ago, the poet John Donne captured the essence of such despairing messages. "Tis all in pieces," he lamented, "all coherence gone."

Finding a Reason for Your Suffering

Our hunger for meaning is never more urgent than during a crisis. When disaster strikes, most people feel an insistent need to explain it. In our own way, each of us has been moved at times to ask the question posed by the long-suffering Ukrainian Hasidic rabbi, Levi Yitzhak of Berdichev: "Lord of the world," he cried, "show me one thing: Show me what this, which is happening at this very moment, means to me." Psychologist Aaron Antonovsky, in his book *Health, Stress, and Coping*, correctly maintains that human suffering is most intolerable when it is inexplicable. We do not wish to fall, in the words of the poet Wallace Stevens, "as apples fall, without astronomy."

Studies of individuals under severe stress show that when we can identify a rationale for our anguish, our capacity to endure is significantly increased. Washington psychiatrist Paul Chodoff and a team of investigators have described, for example, how parents of children with leukemia managed to cope with their ordeal. "They took comfort," the researchers report, "in the thought that the treatment administered to their child, even though bound to fail, would contribute to scientific progress . . . and thus to the saving of some other child in the future." In another study, bereaved couples who coped after the death of their baby said they gained some strength by viewing their loss as an opportunity for growth in their own lives; they felt that their relationships had deepened and improved as a result of the tragedy they shared. And in a five-year follow-up of divorced couples, California researchers Judith S. Wallerstein and Joan B. Kelley found that many of their subjects had significantly improved their way of thinking about themselves and their future after the breakup.

People facing even the most horrible experiences imaginable

are fortified by the conviction that their suffering is not altogether without meaning. In his observations of Polish concentration camp survivors, Warsaw psychiatrist Adam Szymusik found a noteworthy pattern. Survivors who had taken no strong convictions into the inferno with them have not fared as well over time as those who felt that they suffered because of the religious or political views they held dear. Psychiatrist Leo Eitinger, himself a concentration camp survivor, also maintains that it was devotion to a higher cause—whether personal or political—that enabled many Nazi death-camp inmates like himself to go on to lead normal lives after their nightmare had ended. "If we have our own *why* of life," wrote the philosopher Nietzsche, "we shall get along with almost any *how*."

In a recent radio interview, survivor Gerta Weissman looked back forty years to her experiences as an inmate of Nazi concentration camps: "You know, when people ask me, 'Why did you go on?' there is only one picture that comes to mind. That moment was when once I stood at the window of the first camp I was in and asked myself probably the most important question of my life. I asked if, by some miraculous power, one wish could be granted to me, what would it be? . . . And then, with almost crystal clarity, the picture came to my mind. And what I saw was a picture at home—my father smoking his pipe, my mother working at her needlepoint, my brother and I doing our homework. And I remember thinking, my God, it was just a boring evening at home. I had known countless evenings like that. And I knew that this picture would be, if I could help it, the driving force to my survival."

Among the 566 POWs who returned from Vietnam, only one committed suicide. At first, Air Force Captain Alan Brudno was ecstatic over his freedom. "Words like unbelievable, exciting and unreal," he said, "perfectly describe this fantastic experience of being reborn." A month later, however, Alan's mood began to change, and ultimately he ended his life with an overdose of sleeping pills. Before Alan died, he wrote in French: "My life is no longer worth living."

What went wrong? Why, after surviving his nightmare of captivity, did he welcome death?

Alan's brother, Robert, later revealed how badly it had wounded the former POW to find on his return that millions of Americans were against the war. Worst of all, Alan came home to discover that his own wife and parents had become antiwar activists. They had totally rejected the cause that took Alan to Vietnam in the first place, and for which he had sacrificed almost a decade of his life. All his suffering, he finally concluded, had been in vain.

In contrast to Alan, Richard A. Stratton is typical of the many stalwart survivors of Vietnam captivity who, to this day, harbor no doubt about the reason for their ordeal. Stratton admits that his long years as a POW meant precious time lost from his wife and children and from the pursuit of his career. "But I don't look at my part in the war as a waste," he says. "It was the right war at the right time, and in the right place. We belonged there, and I continue to believe that my presence there had a meaning for my country."

The impulse to find a consoling logic for our pain is so strong that some people even take comfort in apparently farfetched rationalizations. In attempts to come to terms with the death of their infants, for example, parents have concluded that the baby would have grown up to be physically, intellectually, or morally defective. When a retarded boy drowned in a public pool, grieving lifeguards eventually decided that the victim and his family were actually better off now that he was dead.

In their first conversations with me just hours after their liberation from Iran, many of the American hostages struggled to impose some meaning, however flimsy, on their fourteen disastrous months of captivity. They described the "benefits" of their experience. "Sure, I lost forty pounds, but I'm now down to my normal weight," said one. "I was a two-pack-a-day smoker, but I expected them to take my cigarettes from me so I quit cold," announced another. "One thing captivity taught me: to give up my two-bourbon-a-night habit," said yet another. In their own way, each of these victims seemed comforted, as we all are, to find that even a remote purpose was served by their ordeal.

For a surprising number of people, simply proving that survival is possible lends purpose to their stress. This was the case, in the view of John Limbert, among many of his fellow hostages in Iran. "Foreign service officers have been regarded as softies, you know," says Limbert. "They're supposedly people who live most of their lives on the cocktail circuit and don't really accomplish very much. Now, all of a sudden, they had a sense of mission: to act appropriately and to survive with dignity. This became their source of strength. It gave them a frame of reference by which to judge themselves—a goal to achieve."

Tel Aviv psychologist Nitza Yarom interviewed Israeli soldiers on the effects of their combat experience. Many of the soldiers, she reports, were surprised by their own competence and adaptability during combat, and they grew convinced that they could cope with life stresses better than they had ever suspected. Said one tank commander: "I learned to appreciate myself more. I would not have believed that I was capable of holding out the way I did." The experience increased his sense of self-worth— as it did many of his comrades. "I did not run away. I proved myself," he said.

A similar attitude has been found among many who successfully endure a long and painful illness or injury. In one study, for example, severely burned patients described their injuries as helping to make them better people; their experience, they said, was "a trial by fire or purgatory," and they had somehow proved themselves by living through it. Many decades ago, Henry Wadsworth Longfellow gave poetic voice to this soul-strengthening posture. "It has done me good," Longfellow wrote, "to be somewhat parched by the heat and drenched by the rain of life."

Using Stress as an Excuse— Or an Opportunity

Not long ago, a neighbor—let's call him Martin—lost his wife. She died suddenly of a heart attack while dressing for work. Like most people traumatized by such a sudden and searing loss, Martin suffered for months from a normal grief reaction. He had all the symptoms of depression—including crying spells, insomnia, poor appetite, inability to concentrate, feelings of worthlessness and guilt. He was inconsolable, constantly preoccupied, even in his dreams, with thoughts of his dead wife.

Eventually Martin's acute symptoms passed. The expected period of mourning was over, and it was time to pick up the pieces and start afresh. Martin, who had been working only sporadically, went back to his job, and he began to see friends for dinner and a weekend golf match. But, as everyone soon noticed, Martin had changed. No longer kind and generous, he now sulked constantly and took offense at the most innocent remark. Normally a caring person, Martin now missed appointments without offering an excuse and tossed insults at the slightest provocation.

Last week, after a disastrous dinner, an old friend drew him aside. "Martin, what's ailing you?"

"Are you kidding?" Martin shot back. "Don't you realize what I've been through? If you were in my shoes, you'd act the same way."

Martin was behaving in a fashion typical of those who view the crises they endure as an excuse for giving up. I've met many such people. For them, the rest of life becomes a massive cop-out. They wear their suffering as if it were a victim's badge that allows them the "privilege" of chronic bitterness. "I'm soured on life," one woman, abandoned by her husband, recently admitted to me. "I just don't give a damn." The result is apt to be deteriorating behavior toward others, interrupted careers, scarred marriages, even abusiveness toward children.

There is, in contrast, an infinitely more healing response to our pain and suffering. We can use the crises we endure not as excuses for regression but as opportunities for growth. Consider, for example, the case of Theodore Kessler. At twenty-nine, Kessler, a victim of muscular dystrophy, is confined to a wheelchair. But he has not allowed himself to become a professional victim. Instead, he is moving ahead with a promising medical career.

After being rejected by fifty American medical schools, Kessler earned his degree in the Dominican Republic. Friends had to carry his wheelchair up several flights of stairs every day so that he could attend classes. Because his illness causes degeneration of the muscles, routine medical tasks such as taking a patient's blood pressure are impossible. He cannot dress himself or open a door. But Dr. Kessler has refused to view his continuing ordeal as the occasion for withdrawal and despair. Instead, he sees it as an opportunity to inspire others.

As a resident, beginning his training at New York's Metropolitan Hospital, Dr. Kessler's day begins at 8:00 A.M. and often ends thirty-four hours later. His patients are the sickest of the mentally ill. And they are obviously fond of him. When he wheels himself through the ward, they often greet him by name. "Dr. Kessler is interested in what's really wrong," says a twenty-five-year-old man suffering from schizophrenia. One woman, long obsessed with fears of being ruled by the devil, momentarily loses her terror. "I see you work so hard," she says to Kessler admiringly. "Where does your strength come from?"

Kessler is aware that his patients respond differently to him than to other doctors. "I don't think about it," he says. "I'm too busy." He is energized by the chance to "make a real dent in these people's lives." And he hopes to someday specialize in treating patients who also have physical handicaps.

Kessler is not alone in using his personal ordeal to give meaning to life. Commander Ralph E. Gaither, for example, was shot down over North Vietnam in October 1965. Gaither spent his first fourteen months as a POW in solitary and later endured daily beatings, starvation, and weeks in an underground "bomb shelter" where he was forced to stand, ankle deep, in human excrement. When he was finally released in 1973, it would have been understandable for him to put that nightmare entirely behind him.

Instead, he did the opposite. Resuming his life as a naval officer, he began working toward a degree in sociology. Gaither wanted to pass on to others the insights he had acquired about resisting breakdown as a POW so that they would not have to be discovered afresh in the future. Gaither's years of suffering as a captive have given direction and meaning to his new life as a free man. "I was a young ensign when I was captured," he said, "and I came home almost eight years later as a lieutenant commander with no expertise other than being a survivor. I decided to devote the remainder of my career to survival training." Since his release, Gaither has directed and guided such a program for the Navy in Pensacola, Florida.

Gaither was incarcerated by a military enemy. In the case of thirty-five-year-old Sandy Martin, an intelligent and creative schoolteacher, the enemy was within. Eight years ago, Sandy began to show the unmistakable signs of mental illness. Her colleagues began to notice erratic and irresponsible behavior. Suddenly she would go on a strange high, shouting and laughing constantly, always interrupting others, often using foul language. Her thoughts became disconnected, jumping from one idea to another without logic. She was perpetually on the move, dreaming up ludicrous projects and recklessly spending all of her savings. At home, she could not sleep or rest. Often in the middle of the night she would get dressed and go out shopping in the darkness, or telephone stunned friends for a 3:00 A.M. chat.

After a few days, however, Sandy would plummet into a depression so deep that she was immobilized. "Suddenly," she recalls, "I had nothing to live for. I had no interests, no goals, no feelings except despair. Each day was a wasteland, and I was obsessed with plans for killing myself."

Doctors diagnosed Sandy as a victim of manic-depressive illness, a devastating mood disorder caused by chemical disturbances in the brain. She spent more than six months in a mental hospital where, with the help of the drug lithium, she recovered. She would have to continue on the drug indefinitely, her doctors told her, to stave off future episodes.

When Sandy returned to society, she was determined not to let her ordeal block her future. On the contrary, she decided to use her experience as a stepping-stone to a new career. She went back to school and recently received her doctorate as a clinical psychologist. Her innovative treatment program for students overwhelmed by stress and suffering from depression is fast being adopted in colleges across the country.

"I'm happy now that I fell apart," says Sandy. "It was the best education I could have had for my career in the field of mental health. I already know what it's like to feel stigmatized by emotional breakdown. I don't need a book to tell me what black depression and screaming anxiety are like. The students who depend on me know that because of what I had to battle and overcome, I will be better able to help them win their battles as well." Using her ordeal as an opportunity has given Sandy a new existence. "I can look forward now to a useful life," she says. "The terrible void has been filled."

Some people have been able to sustain themselves by actually planning for their future while still at the height of their ordeal. The most extreme suffering was for them, in Erich Fromm's words, "the midwife of change." Such was the case for Frankl when he arrived in Auschwitz. Except for his sister, his entire family perished. Every possession lost, everything he valued destroyed, hungry, cold, always expecting death, how could he still want to live?

Frankl's answer: His trials were endurable because he looked toward a time when they would assume significance. He was using his experience to develop logotherapy, a new system of psychotherapy that would eventually help others find some meaning and consolation in their own life crises. In his book, *Man's Search for Meaning*, Frankl describes how, in the cold and dark of his Auschwitz ordeal, he imagined himself lecturing in a warm, well-lit room. The topic of his imaginary lecture was "The Psychology of the Concentration Camp."

Like Frankl, many captives have experienced their ordeal as an opportunity. They used their time in prison to teach themselves new languages, learn new skills, write poetry or books, or lay out plans for the years ahead. "The perspectives of a prison cell give a unique dimension to the past," one returnee observed, "and hopefully it can contribute to the future."

One POW returned from Vietnam without the alcohol problem that had scarred his life for years. As a captive, he made significant career decisions and could now pursue his goals with a determination never before evident. Another claimed: "I can now see so much to be grateful for. Things that I have taken for granted are so much more precious to me." His goal, he said, was "to sift out those things that are most important and to reduce my lifetime to what really matters."

Moorhead Kennedy, taken hostage in Iran and now executive director of the Council on International Understanding, recently described his experience in this way: "I came out of the hostage experience a very different person. My wife said, 'One Kennedy went over there, and another one came back.' She said afterward that she rather preferred the one that came back. It brought out of me things I didn't know I had. I wouldn't recommend this—but I'm glad that I went through it."

These are hardly isolated cases. Countless "victims" report that they were strengthened rather than diminished by their experiences. They insist that they are wiser, more content, and know themselves and the world about them better. "I have a more comprehensive view of the world now; I see things from all angles," said one of the Israeli soldiers interviewed by Yarom. "I learned to differentiate between the more important and the less important things," said another. "The war changed me a lot. There is in me much more self-awareness, openness, desire to look more significantly into significant things," observed still another.

Yarom's study shows how crises can induce a more tolerant and deeper relationship with others. One of the combat soldiers she interviewed put it this way: "When your life is in perpetual danger, when you see how meaningless you are, you learn to appreciate other people, to be less critical of them." Said another veteran: "I am closer to people. People are closer to me."

Shlomo Breznitz, who directs a stress research center at Haifa University, is convinced that we have too long ignored the opportunities that stress presents. "The basic realization of the human condition—that one's days are numbered—has a far-reaching impact on most of us." Misfortune often gives us a rare opportunity to see ourselves in true perspective. "During exposure to stress," writes Breznitz, "it is often easier to separate the essential from the secondary, the important from the unimportant, the signal from the noise."

Gerta Weissman recalls an episode one spring when she and her fellow concentration camp inmates stood roll call for hours on end, nearly collapsing with hunger and fatigue. "We noticed in the corner of this bleak, horrid, gray place that the concrete had broken in a corner and a flower had poked its head through it. And you would see thousands of feet shuffle every morning to avoid stepping on that flower. You know, I don't suggest a stay in a concentration camp for appreciation of art and beauty, but there were incredible moments there."

The crises we encounter, it is clear, can often help to reveal a meaningful focus in our lives—a flower growing through the concrete. Indeed, such a revelation is possible even when the end of life's journey is at hand.

Discovering Life in the Face of Death

In his book, *Dialogue with Death*, Abraham Schmitt describes a patient who, following a period on renal dialysis, survived a kidney transplant and began life again. Here is how she describes her experience:

> . . . I think of myself as having lived two lives. I even call them the first and the second Kathy. The first Kathy died during dialysis. . . . A second Kathy had to be born. This is the Kathy that was born in the midst of death. . . . The first Kathy was a frivolous kid. She lived only one minute at a time.

She quibbled about cold food in the cafeteria, about the bore-dom of surgical nursing lectures, about the unfairness of her parents. . . . The future was far away and of little concern. She lived for trivia only.

But the second Kathy—that's me now. I am infatuated with life. Look at the beauty in the sky! It's gorgeously blue! I go into a flower garden, and every flower takes on such fabulous colors that I am dazzled by their beauty. . . . One thing I do know, had I remained my first Kathy. . . . I would never have known what the real joy of living was all about. I had to face death eyeball to eyeball before I could live. I had to die in order to live.

The case is hardly unique. Countless people reclaimed from death—or living with the knowledge that the end is near—find new and transforming meaning in life. A man who had cancer of the mouth in his early forties decided to spend more time at home with his family and eventually gave up his position for a less demanding one. A nurse who was doggedly pursuing a Ph.D. fulfilled an old fantasy of traveling around the world. A young man with testicular cancer decided to get married and return to school. Psychiatrist Stephen B. Shanfield describes such cases as "the creative use of the crisis of illness."

Many of the Israeli soldiers interviewed by Yarom after the Yom Kippur War of 1976 reported that they now saw life as truly precious. Said one of the soldiers: "My attitude toward death did not change. My attitude toward life changed. . . . Today I appreciate life enormously. I have a fantastic desire to live." Another said: "I want to take more advantage of life, to enjoy more. I look around more, I pay more attention instead of always being in a hurry."

Yalom, who has worked for many years with terminally ill

cancer patients, is struck by "how many of them use their crisis and their danger as an opportunity for change." He has observed startling shifts in their priorities and agendas, massive inner changes that he characterizes as nothing short of "personal growth." These victims have sought to give fresh meaning to their lives. Finally liberated to choose not to do those things they did not wish to do, they rearranged their priorities. They began to live fully in the present rather than postponing life until retirement or some other time in the future. They were now able to communicate more deeply with loved ones than they did before they were stricken. They shed their debilitating fears and concerns about rejection and were suddenly willing to take risks. And they enjoyed a vivid appreciation of the "elemental facts of life"—the changing seasons, the wind, falling leaves, the last Christmas.

Many cancer patients, despite their pain, describe a newly discovered capacity to attend to the essentials of life. "I have much more enjoyment of each day, each moment," said one. "I am not so worried about what is or what isn't or what I wish I had. All those things you get entangled with don't seem to be part of my life right now." Another put it this way: "You just take a long look at your life and realize that many things you thought were important before are totally insignificant . . . . You find out that things like relationships are really the most important things you have—the people you know and your family— everything else is just way down the line."

Shortly before his death from cancer, Senator Richard Neuberger portrayed the remarkable transformations he experienced:

> "A change came over me which I believe is irreversible. Questions of prestige, of political success, of financial status, became all at once unimportant. . . . I never thought of my seat in the Senate, of my bank account, or the destiny of the

free world. My wife and I have not had a quarrel since my illness was diagnosed. . . .

In their stead has come a new appreciation of things I once took for granted—eating lunch with a friend, scratching Muffet's ears and listening for his purrs, the company of my wife, reading a book or magazine in the quiet cone of my bed lamp at night, raiding the refrigerator for a glass of orange juice or a slice of coffee cake. For the first time I think I am actually savoring life . . . I shudder when I remember all the occasions that I spoiled for myself—even when I was in the best of health—by false pride, synthetic values, and fancied slights."

Sigmund Freud made a similar reassessment. In 1926, Freud developed heart trouble on top of his agonizing ordeal with the cancer that was eroding his mouth and jaw. Returning to Vienna from a sanitorium, he asked to be taken for morning drives. For the first time, he said, he experienced the glories of springtime in Vienna. "What a pity," he wrote, "that one has to grow old and ill before making this discovery."

In his career in the Senate, Jacob Javits was known as a workaholic. "I'm still a workaholic," he says, "but there's one big difference now. Before, my life was so busy that I was constantly going on to something else, but now I really have an opportunity to enjoy communicating with my wife and my children and my family—and as my wife, Marion, so aptly puts it: Now I really *see* them. This is a wonderful pleasure—and one of the compensations which my disability has imposed, but which, I think, has broadened my life and given it an added dimension."

In October 1983, Massachusetts Senator Paul Tsongas, only half as old as Javits, discovered that he has nodular lymphoma, a form of cancer that, though not immediately fatal, will probably allow him to live only about eight more years. Soon after his condition was diagnosed, Tsongas abandoned his meteoric political career, returning home to New England with his wife, Niki, and their three daughters. "The illness made me face up to the fact that I will die someday," writes Tsongas. "It made me think about wanting to look back without regret whenever that happened. It made me appreciate Niki's strengths as I had never quite done before. I am blessed with a marriage that provides meaning. I would now look at my wife and see her in a way one does not in the rush of everyday life."

Reading these accounts stirred in me recollections of the precious mornings I sat beside my dying brother Shalom, listening to Mahler symphonies. For many years before he developed cancer, Shalom was enmeshed in seemingly endless turmoil about his family, his work, and his precarious finances. His frenetic days and sleepless nights allowed no time for quiet contemplation, no moments of repose. But now, facing death, he was finding nuances in life that he had never fully savored. "I've always loved music," he confided, "but I've never really heard it the way I do now."

Elizabeth Kubler-Ross, whose career was devoted to easing the human confrontation with death, took note of the remarkable meanings that dying patients, young and old, attached to their lives. "Not one of them has ever told me how many houses she had or how many handbags or sable coats," wrote Kubler-Ross. "What they tell you are very tiny, almost insignificant moments of their lives—where they went fishing with a child, or they tell of the mountain-climbing trips to Switzerland. Some brief moments in an interpersonal relationship. These are the things that keep people going to the end. . . . They remember little moments that they had long forgotten, and they suddenly have a smile on their faces. And they begin to reminisce about little memories that make their whole life meaningful and worthwhile.

I never understood in forty years what the church tried to teach—that there is meaning in suffering—until I found myself in this situation."

Filling the Void

Few people are able to sustain themselves in the face of crisis only with the belief that "It is God's will"—that there is a higher purpose in human suffering that we cannot perceive. Only rare—and fortunate—individuals find serenity simply by accepting their lot with equanimity and perfect faith.

Most of us must find meaning, instead, in the day-to-day activities of our lives. Barbara Gordon, who fought her way back from addiction to Valium and a mental collapse, says: "Each person has his own safe place—running, painting, swimming, fishing, weaving, gardening. The activity itself is less important than the act of drawing on your own resources, talents, and abilities. Meager and threadbare as you may think these are, it is in the *doing* of something meaningful to you that you are enriched; it fills the emptiness that is so much a part of loss."

The therapeutic answer to a world seemingly bereft of meaning, in the view of Yalom, is "engagement"—finding something that captures our attention and pursuing it passionately. Wholehearted involvement in any of life's activities, he insists, not only rids us of doubts about the ultimate meaning of life but increases the possibility that we will complete the pattern of events in our lives in a coherent and meaningful fashion. "To find a home, to care about other individuals, about ideas or projects, to search, to create, to build—these, and all other forms of engagement . . . are intrinsically enriching," says Yalom.

To fill the void left by our losses, it is not necessary, in other words, for us to discover that elusive, ultimate, cosmic meaning of life. We need only find meaning in what we do today, tonight. We need, according to Yalom, to invent our own meaning rather than to discover God's or nature's meaning.

A decade ago, as my brother Jack's life began to ebb after a five-year struggle with leukemia, he received a letter from Edith Samuels, whose husband, the writer Maurice Samuels, had himself died a year earlier. "Moish," as Edith called her husband, had been my brother's friend, and she was reminding Jack of his dogged insistence on working every day, despite the physical obstacles:

> I think of Moish in the last decade, meeting all his lecture engagements, even against doctor's orders, once even traveling across the country with a doctor and wheelchair at every stop. I think of Moish pushing his way, literally pushing, through his book *In Praise of Yiddish*, getting up every single morning to come to his desk. I think of him in the last year, and in the last week and the last *days*, slowly, slowly, slowly writing by hand in the hospital. As long as he lived, he said, as long as God would give him strength, he would work, because what was the purpose of his creation, if he did not work? He was always very stern with me if I pleaded that he stop working. *That*, he said, was unthinkable. As long as he breathed, he would work. . . . Take good care, Jack. And keep in good spirits. And remember: every day of work is a triumph over illness.

My brother lived that message to the very end. I remember sitting at his bedside as the clear, crisp days of October ushered in the Jewish New Year season. Throughout his career as a rabbi, this was for Jack the high point of the calendar—the time for crafting sermons that he would thunder to a full house of worshipers. Now he lay in a hospital bed, his face hollowed by the disease in him, his skin barely masking the skeleton beneath. At his side was a note pad and pen. From time to time, he awoke from his dozing and scribbled notes for the Yom Kippur message he wanted—no, literally planned—to deliver to his flock.

On the eve of Yom Kippur, the setting sun brought the annual surge of worshipers to the congregation to hear once again the ancient cantillations of the Kol Nidre prayer. The news spread quickly. The rabbi had died hours earlier. He had left them peacefully, working to fill the void in his life—and theirs.

Self-contempt, bitterer to drink than blood.
PERCY BYSSHE SHELLEY
Prometheus Unbound II

4.
A Clear Conscience: Shedding Self-Blame

A few year ago, a government-wide budget cut forced me to reduce by a third the size of my office staff. I had to tell twenty employees that the jobs they held were no longer theirs. The grounds used to determine who these people would be—length of service in the federal government and whether or not they happened to be military veterans—had nothing to do with their personal characteristics or performance. Yet on hearing the news, many of the affected staff members assumed personal responsibility for their fate.

"I guess if I were a different kind of person," said one, "I wouldn't be in this fix." And a secretary, always a model of efficiency and productivity, admonished herself: "I'm sure if I had done better work, I would have been saved." Few of the stricken employees could accept my assurances that their loss was due entirely to forces outside themselves.

The impulse to feel accountable for our suffering surfaces in early childhood and persists throughout our lives. In their book on the experience of hospitalized children, pediatric nurse Madeline Petrillo and pediatrician Siray Sanger describe Danny, a two-year-old leukemia victim. As the nurse pierced his tiny arm with an intravenous needle to begin still another painful round of chemotherapy, he screamed over and over again, "I'm sorry; I said I'm sorry," convinced that his pain was punishment for something he had done. In 1976, twenty-six California children were kidnapped at gunpoint by three masked men who took over the school bus on which they were riding. The victims were buried in a hole, which was actually a truck trailer placed underground and covered with a layer of earth. After sixteen hours, the kidnappers finally left and the terrorized children dug themselves out. One child, eleven-year-old Sheila, had argued bitterly with her mother on the morning of the kidnapping, and she had left for school screaming, "You're the meanest mother in the world!" For years afterward, Sheila linked that parting shot with her subsequent trauma. Another child, fourteen-year-old Bob, dawdled so much that morning that his mother, instead of driving as usual, ordered him to take the bus. In Bob's mind, the logic was clear: the kidnapping was his punishment.

Similar guilt reactions are displayed by innocent youngsters caught in the crossfire of their parents' divorce ("If only I'd behaved better, Mom and Dad would have gotten along"); brilliant students turned down by overcrowded colleges ("I was stupid—I should have studied harder"); people who become seriously ill, suffer an accident, fall victim to crime, or watch a mate die.

As we will see later, assuming personal responsibility when misfortune strikes can sometimes serve a useful purpose, motivating us to set our lives aright. But chronic self-recrimination leads to malignant hopelessness that is certain to limit our capacity to prevail over stress.

Unfortunately, it is just such a blanket indictment that we tend to inflict on ourselves in the face of catastrophic events. Research on experiences as different as facing a divorce, losing a job, developing cancer, and being raped, shows that we often suffer a badly tarnished self-image even when we bear no conceivable responsibility for our fate.

The result can be a retreat from others who might offer support. Feeling unworthy of help, we withdraw even from close friends and family. Clearly, our penchant for self-demolishing blame in the face of stress must be understood and overcome if we are to emerge from life's traumas unvanquished.

Why Guilt Comes Naturally

On the face of it, feeling guilty for your own suffering seems perverse. Why would anyone, already wounded by events, accept the role of accomplice? There are two reasons.

To begin with, we are taught from earliest childhood that we will be punished for disobedience or failure. ". . . if ye will not hearken unto me, I will do this unto you: I will appoint terror over you, even consumption and fever, that shall make the eyes to fail and the soul to languish. And I will make your cities a waste, and will bring the land into desolation . . ." Underlying our religious and moral traditions are thunderous Old Testament warnings such as these. Small wonder that when things go badly, we assume that the pain is a God-given punishment.

A few months ago, newly widowed Karen told me about the remorse she felt over the death of her husband. Her marriage of twenty-one years to Marty was often turbulent. Because they were both headstrong and fiercely independent, they had repeated confrontations. But they also enjoyed an underlying affection and loyalty toward each other, and their marriage endured.

It has been nearly two years since Marty died after a sudden heart attack, and Karen continues to feel certain that she is being punished for having been "an uncompromising bitch." She blames his death—and her own bereavement—squarely on herself. The other day she remembered a comment Marty used to make when he was especially exasperated. "Karen," he would say, "you're going to be the death of me."

"And that's exactly what I was," moans Karen, who now suffers such depression she can hardly get out of bed on some mornings. She views herself as worthless and her future as hopeless.

Even crime victims fall into an emotional trap like Karen's, associating their misfortune with some earlier and totally unrelated "bad" behavior. One man who was the target of a robbery, for example, decided that the robber had punished him for quarreling with his wife that morning—as if the criminal were the agent of some higher moral force.

A startling number of physically abused women feel a sense of personal blame. Somehow, they conclude, they must have provoked their husbands' brutal attacks. Victims of incest frequently believe that if they had been "better" people, their relatives would not have violated them. And most surprising, victims of crime appear equally ready to take the rap for their predicament. They frequently manage to identify something they did that made it possible for the criminal to succeed. The unlocked window enticed the burglar; the wallet in an outside pocket attracted the pickpocket; the short skirt incited the rapist. One woman, described by Morton Bard and Dawn Sangrey in *The Crime Victim's Book*, blamed herself when her purse was snatched as she waited for a bus. She had known that the neighborhood might be dangerous, but she didn't have the money for a taxi.

"I took the chance and I got caught," she said. "I feel responsible in that I did something I knew I shouldn't have done."

But in addition to our instinctive, eye-for-an-eye view of life, there is a second reason for assuming blame in the face of misfortune: It helps to satisfy our need to believe that we are in control of our own destiny. In effect, you make an emotional trade-off. You accept the idea that you are responsible for yesterday's misfortunes and thereby earn the right to believe that you are in command of all your tomorrows.

The Navy pilots shot down and taken prisoner in Vietnam quickly convinced themselves that had they not "screwed up"— had they not strayed from the flight path, or taken greater precautions—they would not have been captured. By believing that they were responsible for their fate, they could believe as well that their future was not entirely out of their hands. For months after the administrators of my agency launched their unwarranted investigation of me, I was similarly dogged by the notion that the crisis I faced was my own doing. Although it was obvious that I was the victim of the manipulations of others, I could not rid myself of the nagging idea that I was to blame for my plight. Now, in retrospect, the source of that self-blame is clear to me. Like the pilots suddenly enslaved in their POW cells, I desperately needed to feel that I was still in control of my life.

Interestingly, there is evidence that—up to a point—the attitude of self-blame in a crisis can be helpful. A series of recent studies show that accepting some responsibility for a traumatic event may lead to more effective recovery—for example, among women who have been raped, accident victims, and people with a physical illness. Even victims of a technological disaster, such as the radiation accident at Three Mile Island, were found to suffer less stress if they saw themselves as accountable for some of the problems they subsequently experienced. Evidently, a sense of personal liability can make us feel less vulnerable.

And, indeed, such an assessment is sometimes quite valid. "Sometimes we *have* caused the sorrow in our lives," writes Kushner, "and ought to take responsibility." Says psychiatrist Edward Hornick of New York's Albert Einstein College of Medicine: "Guilt is a useful thing to have around because it clues you into what's going on in your life that isn't the way you want it to be." When our guilt feelings are logical and realistic, we can take various kinds of positive action to overcome them.

But there is a world of difference between accepting responsibility for your actions and running yourself down altogether. The second kind of self-blame—the kind that indicts your character rather than your behavior—is no longer a platform for positive action but the breeding ground for hopelessness and depression. University of Massachusetts psychologist Ronnie Janoff-Bulman distinguishes between these two types of self-blame in this way: One person might say, "This happened because I did something which led to it." But another person might say, "This happened to me because I'm the sort of person to whom such things happen." In one case, we place blame only on an act of behavior, while in the other case, we indict our basic character.

There is evidence that the outcome is quite different in each case. Researchers recently interviewed forty-two women who had undergone a mastectomy following a diagnosis of breast cancer, asking them to offer a causal explanation for their illness. The women who felt that their cancer was the result of some specific, earlier behavior believed that they were now free of the disease. Moreover, they were not burdened by depression. In contrast, those who saw their cancer as being in some way related to a basic defect in their personality were in quite a different psychological boat. They believed they still had cancer, and they were depressed.

If unchecked, our natural tendency to blame ourselves for our suffering becomes, as in Karen's case, unreasonable and immobilizing. The danger is especially great because our readiness to indict ourselves is often reinforced by the attitudes of people around us.

The Victim's Stains: How Society Punishes "Losers"

On the night of March 21, 1983, in a seedy tavern in New Bedford, Massachusetts, a group of men seized a young mother, dragged her across the barroom floor, and hoisted her onto a pool table. Holding her down, they pulled off her jeans, stripped her, and forced her to perform oral sex. The victim screamed and begged for help, but no one made a move to rescue her. The leering, laughing onlookers are said simply to have cheered.

The ghastliness of the event was more than matched a year later when the defendants—six young Portuguese immigrants—came to trial in Fall River, Massachusetts. During the month-long courtroom proceedings, televised by both local and national cable-television networks, the victim faced relentless questioning by defense attorneys who attacked her character and moral integrity while trying to undermine her credibility. She was portrayed as a welfare cheat, an unmarried mother who hardly stopped to put her two young children to bed before going out to drink, and a flirt who had actually encouraged the men to violate her.

The case, while extreme, is hardly unique. Society often turns the tables on rape victims out of the widely held belief that the woman is somehow culpable. Harvard psychologist Steven Berglas points out that lawyers defending alleged rapists have long understood that "trying the victim"—portraying her as a provocateur—is an excellent defense strategy. And, indeed, many of the spectators packed into the courtroom to watch the Big Dan's trial were convinced that the victim must have led the men on, or that she had no business going unescorted into the bar.

"Nobody came right out and said it, of course," observed Darlene Wheeler, a New Bedford feminist leader who carefully followed the trial. "But the implications . . . were quite clear: She was asking for it."

Our impulse to blame the sufferer may be most obvious in the case of rape victims, but we tend to do the very same thing to others as well. Society, it seems, just does not like losers. It stands ready, in the words of sociologist Erving Goffman, to reduce the suffering individual "from a whole and usual person to a tainted, discounted one." People who have been victims of a mental disorder or of alcoholism are often viewed as being personally responsible for illness, and even though they have fully recovered, they tend to run into difficulty in landing jobs or places to live. Recovered cancer patients are frequently viewed as "poor risks" for employment. And hostile and rejecting attitudes are surprisingly common as well toward the aged or those with physical disabilities.

Even children are not immune. In the spring of 1974, an Israeli development known as Ma'alot was attacked by three armed terrorists. They occupied a school for sixteen hours, and before the agony was over, twenty-two children had been killed and fifty more wounded.

When the survivors eventually returned to school, they were greeted with surprising hostility. The school authorities cruelly ignored their physical and emotional needs. For example, some of the female victims, embarrassed by their disfigurement, felt obliged to wear slacks to cover the wounds on their legs—but because this form of dress was against the school's rules, they were expelled from class and prohibited from participating in social events. Other students, who found it next to impossible to concentrate, were accused of taking advantage of their experience.

The children's peers were equally unsympathetic. They "looked at us as if we were pariahs," complained one of the girls. Another survivor said: "I wish they knew how it feels to be captured by terrorists, then maybe they would stop ridiculing and bullying me over my amputated arm." And here is the rueful observation of one fourteen-year-old: "Children call us names; they think we are bragging whenever we try to talk about what happened. . . . They call us 'chickens' when we show signs of fear. Had they been there. . . ."

Why do we behave in such a punitive fashion toward the very people who are most vulnerable?

According to University of Waterloo psychologist Melvin J. Lerner, our tendency to blame sufferers is very much like our own self-blame. Both stem from our need to believe in a just world. Our reasoning, according to New York psychiatrist Martin Symonds, goes something like this: "If you act right, nothing wrong will happen; something wrong happened, therefore you weren't acting right."

By censuring the sufferer in this way, Harold Kushner points out, we are able to make evil seem more rational and less threatening. "Blaming the victim," he writes, "is a way of reassuring ourselves that the world is not as bad a place as it may seem, and that there are good reasons for people's suffering. It helps fortunate people believe that their good fortune is deserved, rather than being a matter of luck." Threatened by the possibility that catastrophes can befall good people like ourselves, a surprising number of us decide that victims of misfortune are simply bad people.

Moreover, by stigmatizing those in crisis, we manage to create a safe distance between us and them. It is only a short leap from viewing victims as different from other people—especially you—

to the judgment that they are undeserving of our sympathy. In effect, we can say to the sufferer, "You are responsible for your own troubles, so I don't have to help you." The result, it turns out, can be incredibly heartless behavior toward those who need not censure but support.

Rejecting Those in Need

A free-lance writer using the pseudonym Sigrid Linscott has described how friends retreated from her and her husband when their child suddenly became desperately ill.

> "After initial expressions of sympathy, they drew back from us, and I am still trying to understand why. . . . Were we shunned because of a kind of primitive revulsion against sickness? Were we feared as somehow contagious? (Contagion was not possible.) Were we judged, like Job by his comforters, to have committed a great sin, since we had incurred such punishment? Or were we simply unwelcome reminders of mortality, of the precariousness of life? The lessons we have wrested from this year—that safety is an illusion, that humans have much less control over life than they think—may be unbearable for some people. And why bear them, secondhand, if you don't have to?"

Physician David Rabin, a victim of Lou Gehrig's disease, described how fellow doctors turned him into a nonperson.

> By the fall of 1979, I was walking with a limp; I countered the queries I received in every corridor by saying I had a "disk." This was not threatening to my colleagues, who proffered advice on how to deal with it and regaled me with their own

back problems. I was still a full member of the fraternity, in excellent standing. By early 1980, however, the limp was worse, and I now held a cane in my right hand. The inquiries ceased and were replaced by a very obvious desire to avoid me. When I arrived at work in the morning I could see, from the corner of my eye, colleagues changing their pace or stopping in their tracks to spare themselves the embarrassment of bumping into me. . . . As the cane became inadequate and was replaced by a walker, so my isolation from my colleagues intensified. . . . One day, while crossing the little courtyard outside the emergency room, I fell. A longtime colleague was walking by. He turned, and our eyes met as I lay sprawled on the ground. He quickly averted his eyes, pretended not to see me, and continued walking. He never even broke stride. I suppose he ignored the obvious need for help out of embarrassment and discomfort, for I know him to be a compassionate and caring physician. . . .

Rabin's disheartening experience at the hands of a fellow physician may seem exceptional, but it is not. Victims of misfortune often end up being hurt by the very doctors, nurses, and police officers who should logically be the first to provide comfort and support. To protect themselves emotionally—and to separate themselves from the tainted sufferer—they often assume an aloof and remote attitude toward those in need. The result is described by Symonds as a "second injury"—the salt of rejection poured on top of already painful emotional wounds.

A surprising number of doctors inflict such an injury on patients suffering from so-called self-induced illnesses—alcoholism, anxiety, depression. As an experiment, one man visited thirty-two doctors and complained of ulcer symptoms. He told half of them, however, that he had a history of emotional illness.

These doctors, it turned out, were less inclined to accept the complaints of their patient and viewed him as being less in need of medical attention than did the others.

When the bureaucratic overlords launched their investigation into my alleged wrongdoing, I soon became aware that many of my associates—fellow members of the mental health professions—were beginning to keep themselves at a safe distance. They were finding it difficult to identify with someone who was now blemished and vulnerable. In the same vein, I remember an airplane conversation with Daniel Ellsberg, whose indictment for releasing the Pentagon papers to *The New York Times* drew him into a debilitating and financially exhausting court trial. The hardest thing about those years, he told me, was being abandoned by friends and associates. "No one ever dropped by or called to say 'How are you doing?' " Ellsberg said. And his own telephone calls often went unreturned.

The consequences for the targets of such rejecting attitudes can be devastating—as is abundantly evident among many veterans of the Vietnam War. During the dozen years since they returned from that experience, these men have suffered an avalanche of post-traumatic stress symptoms. Anxiety, depression, sleep disorders, and alcoholism are so common among them that the Veterans Administration has been forced to set up a national network of storefront counseling programs to help stem the tide.

These symptoms, I am convinced, have been perpetuated— in some cases even caused—by the guilt trip laid on Vietnam veterans by their fellow Americans. Rather than being honored for their sacrifice when they returned, they were treated as rejects and failures. Popular stereotypes of Vietnam veterans as wild and dangerous misfits—all nurtured in the popular media—have helped to deface the self-concepts of the returning warriors. David E. Bonoir and his colleagues, in their book *The Vietnam Veteran;*

A History of Neglect, describe the second injury we inflicted on these vets. "When the war ended, quarreling U.S. institutions did not carry their dead home from the battlefield, offered no dignity to their wounded, but simply withdrew, leaving those whom they implicitly regarded as irrelevant to make their own way home."

Interestingly, one group of returnees from Vietnam—the former POWs—seem to be doing unusually well, despite the fact that there was good reason to expect just the opposite. Here were men, as described throughout this book, who were subjected to brutal and prolonged stress. It would have been natural for them to suffer a host of physical and psychological problems upon their return. Yet a follow-up study by San Diego psychologist Milton Richlin and his associates reveal these liberated prisoners to be healthier and less likely to be depressed than Vietnam veterans who never endured captivity.

The explanation must in part lie in the contrasting receptions given the two groups by their countrymen when they returned from their respective ordeals. The POWs, unlike their combat-scarred comrades, were treated with honor and admiration, feted by President Nixon and wildly cheered in parades by ticker-tape crowds. Small wonder that they have apparently developed fewer symptoms than their stigmatized comrades, many of whom, according to a number of studies, experienced such overwhelming feelings of shame that they went to great lengths to keep their role in Vietnam a secret. As one veteran put it: "I've still got to hide the fact that I was in that mess. People just don't understand what we went through. They still blame us."

Each of us—veterans of suffering in our own way—must resist the tendency to accept society's blame for our personal misfortunes. In denying that verdict, the most potent weapon available to us is a spirit of defiance—even outrage and anger. Those who conquer the crises in their lives do not retreat in disgrace. Instead, they develop a tenacity born of the belief that their ordeal is not an end but a beginning.

Substituting Grit for Guilt

Bree Walker's hands and feet are severely deformed as a result of a rare birth defect, *syndactylism* commonly known as "webbed hands and feet." Yet Bree is now a successful and widely acclaimed TV news anchor woman in San Diego—a position she achieved only after defiantly rejecting the shame she felt over her condition.

"I'll never forget finding out that boys I dated called me 'gimp' and 'lobster claws' behind my back," she says. In self-defense, Bree even told jokes at her own expense. But that, she soon learned, did nothing to stem the tide of whispers and stares. "Eventually I learned that shame can also be a form of disability—and that I'd just have to try harder to get the things I wanted in life."

What Bree wanted was a career in the limelight. As a little girl, she remembers, she would see her own reflection on the TV screen, all the while devising secret plans for the person she would be when she grew up: "glamorous like Marilyn Monroe, adventurous like Sky King's niece, Penny, and most appealing, bright, and aggressive, like *Daily Planet* reporter Lois Lane."

While studying journalism at the University of Minnesota, Bree decided to become a newspaper reporter. But without typing skills, she was unable to get a typing job. So she enrolled in a broadcasting school, hoping for a career in radio as a disc jockey. Radio was perfect, she thought. "It offered limelight—and visual anonymity." Eventually Bree became New York's first female drive-time DJ at station WYNY. But all the while, deep inside, she never gave up on her eventual goal: a career in television—on that screen that had nourished her childhood fantasies.

Bree worked in radio for nearly eight years before she began to try to sell herself as she was—a talented but deformed reporter. She was determined not to let her weird-looking hands hold her back.

"It was a long struggle," says Bree. "I moved to San Diego because I felt that in a smaller market, my chances of making the crossover from radio to TV would be better. I enrolled in a telecommunications class at San Diego City College, where I managed to do some anchoring on the college TV station, and put some tapes together. I started showing the tapes to the three network affiliates in town, and it took over a year of courting the stations before one of them—KGTV—was actually willing to take a chance."

At first, Bree used a set of rubber prosthetic gloves during her five-minute local newscasts. But eventually the gloves began to seem silly and clumsy. "It was like wearing a mask," says Bree. In April 1981, off they came—for good. "I forgot about my hands and started to prove myself as a newswoman."

Today Bree co-anchors two daily newscasts. She is admired by her listeners and has won prestigious journalism awards. Each day she proves to herself—and her viewers—that winning life's battles means discarding shame and guilt as a response to misfortune and substituting grit and resolve in their stead.

Helen Winter, a classic victim of wife abuse, is learning that lesson slowly. For eight years she has been pummeled, pinched, slapped, and choked by her husband, Ned—a textbook case who compensates for his feelings of inferiority by tyrannizing his wife. Helen is an innocent victim, yet she has continued to serve abjectly as Ned's private punching bag.

Helen's readiness to accept her role as an abused wife is fueled largely by self-blame. She is not alone. Psychologist Sol Charen, during his long career as chief psychologist of a social-service agency in Rockville, Maryland, has seen a surprising number of such cases. "Many abused women conclude that it's all their fault," says Charen. "Of course, it isn't, but that's usually what the man's been telling her, and she seems ready to believe him."

Like many other troubled individuals, for years Helen was unable to take any action that might extricate her from her trap. Instead, she turned her feelings of resentment and anger inward, against herself, looking for the roots of his pathology in her own personality. "I guess he wouldn't treat me this way if I ran the house more efficiently," she said to a friend one day. "I know it makes him mad when dinner isn't ready on time, or the bed isn't made." The result was predictable—deep and unrelenting depression, the kind neatly described by psychiatrist Willard Gaylin as "the bankruptcy of the individual." When we slavishly accept our dismal fate as deserved, we invite despair—moving, in Gaylin's words, "beyond reassurance, beyond comfort."

Just such an aura of desolation hangs over Helen. "Look, I really don't care anymore," she said recently. "My life means nothing to me. I'd just as soon end it all." For Helen, every day has become an obstacle course. Getting up for work, dressing, planning appointments, seem to take energy reserves and will-power that are just not there. Instead of socializing at lunch or coffee breaks, Helen disappears to spend time by herself. If you were her friend and tried to intrude, she might respond with irritation and tears, and your words of advice would probably be heard as threatening. Her dominant moods are melancholy and remorse, not the resolve that might help her to confront her dilemma and take some action.

Helen has finally been persuaded by a friend to join a mutual support group for battered women, where she can learn to over-come her feelings of self-blame—and finally *do* something about her captivity. As one member of the group recently said to her: "You'll never get anywhere if you feel that you are responsible. If it's all your fault, naturally you're going to stay in that mess and try to work it out. You're going to learn what I did at this shelter—that nobody has a right to do this, that it wouldn't matter which woman it was, that you've got nothing to do with it."

This kind of gritty response to adversity is critical for anyone struggling to find their way back from trauma and stress. Crime victims are beginning to prove the point dramatically. Among violated citizens, there has been a healthy trend to make their plight known. "Like other citizen activists," reports writer Mitchell Satchell, "they are marching to the state legislatures. They are demanding not only tougher laws but better financial compensation, the right of victims to testify about the impact of the crime on their lives, and a raft of other reforms."

Dr. Shelley Neiderbach is a good example. She has been victimized twice. Five years after she was attacked and pistol-whipped in her car in Brooklyn, New York, in 1975, she was mugged at knifepoint in the lobby of her apartment building—experiences she has described as "life-changing, life-shattering." One response might have been, like Helen's, to turn her rage inward. She chose instead to express her outrage.

Dr. Neiderbach began to devote herself to counseling other crime victims in New York City, forming a free service that now includes seven psychologists. She has joined dozens of other experts—nearly 200 of them—in developing counseling approaches, fighting for legislation, and helping to develop a field of scientific research that has come to be known as victimology. Says Neiderbach: "This is how I get back. This is how I get even." She is acting on Henry Ward Beecher's bold perception of defeat, which, he said, "turns bone to flint, and gristle to muscle."

Whether or not we respond to our crises with stiffened resolve can make a difference in our very survival. During the Korean War, hundreds of American captives of the Chinese communists perished in prison camps because of a condition later described as "give-up-itis." Unwilling to challenge the efforts of their captors to indoctrinate them, they accepted the enemy's verdict of guilt. Some actually curled up in their cells in the fetal position. They had lost a capacity found to be essential in any encounter with a crisis—the capacity to hope.

Hope and Survival

It is virtually impossible to feel guilty and hopeful at the same time. The act of hoping, Israeli stress expert Shlomo Breznitz points out, takes energy. It means finding something to build on—an unthinkable task if your energies are consumed by remorse. "One has to dwell on the situation, think it over, weave some possible scenarios, tell oneself some stories with happy endings." Breznitz views hope as one of our psychological vital signs. As long as it is present, it means you are putting up some fight.

During the Second World War, 25,000 American soldiers were held captive by the Japanese. Forced to exist under inhumane conditions, many of them died. Others, however, survived and eventually returned home. There was no reason to believe there was a difference in the stamina of these two groups of soldiers. The survivors, however, were different in one major respect: They confidently expected to be released someday. As described by Robins Reader in *Holding On to Hope*, "They talked about the kind of homes they would have, the jobs they would choose, and even described the kind of person they would marry. They drew pictures on the walls to illustrate their dreams. Some even found ways to study subjects related to the kind of career they wanted to pursue. The doctors taken captive even formed medical societies."

This is precisely the behavior that, in our own lives, keeps us forging ahead. It means learning new skills and going after a different job, recovering from devastating illness, building a new family. "It is this kind of hope," writes Reader, "that makes us try a different road if the one we are on is leading nowhere. It is also this kind of hope which sustains us when we are told there is no hope. Because no matter what our ears hear, what really matters is that hope is in our hearts."

Ellen Alterman contracted polio when she was six and has spent most of her life since in a wheelchair. Yet that life has been productive and fulfilling. Over the years, Ellen has persisted in saying "yes" although the world was saying "no."

For someone bedridden until the age of seventeen, a normal education seemed impossible. But not for Ellen. She kept up with school requirements via a bedside telephone hookup with the school. In her senior year in college, Ellen decided she wanted to become a veterinarian, but she was rejected. With her disability, she was told, she could never manage to inject a horse or handle working on a farm as part of her training. So Ellen turned right around and enrolled instead in a graduate program in animal behavior at the University of Maryland. She never missed a class, and after receiving her master's degree, she joined the Food and Drug Administration, where she has served for fifteen years as a distinguished drug researcher in an animal laboratory.

Soon after Ellen began her job, she met Neil, a man who worked in her building. They started dating and fell in love. Before her marriage to Neil, a gynecologist told her emphatically that children were out of the question—even adopted ones. "With all the normal couples wanting children," he said, "it is very unlikely that any adoption agency would consider you or your husband." But about a year after they were married, Ellen and Neil did adopt Sandy, a two-and-a-half-year-old from India, and three years later, Sandy got the little sister she wanted with the arrival of Shana, also from India. The fact that Ellen was in a wheelchair posed no obstacles. "We were a man and a woman who loved each other and greatly wished for a child—and we were eventually judged on that basis," she says.

Ellen considers herself lucky that she never went for counseling in vocational rehabilitation. "I was never in a position of someone saying to me that I really should go into a field just to accommodate my disability. I made a free choice. When I finished my physical therapy at Warm Springs, Georgia, they said. 'Okay, you're on your own. You don't ever have to come back to us.' I was like a bird leaving the nest."

Breznitz is among a growing number of investigators studying how tenacious optimism such as Ellen's may actually increase the survival potential of individuals enduring stress by changing their body chemistry. A hopeful attitude, these researchers believe, can lead to physiological changes that improve the efficiency of the immune system—the body's defense against toxins and disease.

Many investigators now argue that the state of our immune system is more critical in the development of diseases than actual exposure to disease agents such as viruses and bacteria. Some viruses—for example, herpes simplex—are always present in our bodies, but they only become active and cause harm when something goes wrong with our immune system. Similarly, potential cancer cells are believed to be constantly circulating in our bloodstreams—but in healthy persons, they are routinely eliminated by the immune system. Says Breznitz: "Thoughts, expectations and hopes affect the body's stress reactions more than the actual stressful experience itself."

Can hopeful attitudes affect recovery from disease as well?

One study suggests that how women view their breast cancer may have a greater impact on recovery than the size of the tumor and the type of treatment. And in his book on the characteristics of cancer survivors, Curtis Bill Pepper describes the important role of optimism. A surprising number of those who beat the disease felt they were special. In the words of colon cancer survivor Herman Krevsky: "There was never a moment when I didn't think I was going to make it."

The capacity to nurture an optimistic attitude is obliterated by self-blame. So, too, is the capacity to turn our thoughts outward, toward others. Self-blame means wallowing in private ruminations, cutting ourselves off emotionally from fellow sufferers. And it is precisely this willingness to reach out—to establish sympathetic connections with others in pain—that provides still another important key for winning the toughest battles of our lives.

The best thing you could do was to give when
you had no hope of getting anything in return.
RICHARD A. STRATTON,
former POW in Vietnam

5.
Compassion:
Healing Through
Helping

It was the morning after, and at the hospital in Wies-
baden, Germany, the fifty-two hostages—exhausted by their
ordeal, bewildered by their sudden freedom—began the wrench-
ing process of making contact with the families at home.

They might have been expected to focus on the problems of
their reentry, but instead the hostages turned their attention
away from themselves and focused on others. Their first order
of business was to send a message of sympathy to the families
of the helicopter pilots who had perished in the attempt to rescue
them. Next, the exhausted survivors commandeered a few carts
and organized a team to distribute to their fellow hospital patients
the gifts and flowers sent them from around the world to celebrate
their release. The image is indelible in my mind: the smiling
hostages, a day ago in captivity in Iran, bringing surprise and

delight to other patients with their presents—new mothers, young children, the elderly and infirm.

Easing the Pain by Helping Others

As I watched the bedraggled hostages, it was clear that their act of kindness was as healing to them as to their beneficiaries. Self-absorption and self-pity—natural responses in times of crisis and loss—have never increased anyone's psychological endurance. Instead, compassion for others—turning our attention outward—has been proven to have a remarkable therapeutic effect.

Psychotherapists frequently find that their main task is to help patients shift their focus away from themselves. Viktor Frankl has described a specific technique—he calls it "dereflection"—to divert patients from spending precious time endlessly searching for the neurotic sources of their anxiety and depression. Instead, he directs their attention to the healthier parts of their personalities and encourages them to dwell on the meaningful things they can do and the contributions they can make.

Irvin Yalom agrees that it can be vitally important to get stress-ridden individuals to stop thinking about themselves and to start thinking of others. Group therapy, he finds, is a good place to do this, since self-serving behavior is readily apparent and inevitably becomes an issue among group members. Yalom makes patients responsible for introducing newcomers to the groups and for helping new arrivals to express their anguish and pain to others.

Yalom has seen the most dramatic examples of this process of turning outward to help others in his clinical work with cancer patients. He reports the case of Sal:

Sal was a thirty-year-old patient who had always been vigorous and athletic until he developed multiple myeloma, a painful and disabling form of bone cancer from which he died two years later. In some ways Sal's last two years were the richest of his life. Though he lived in considerable pain and though he was encased in a full body cast (because of multiple bone fractures), Sal found great meaning in life by being of service to many young people. Sal toured high schools in the area counseling teen-agers on the hazards of drug abuse and used his cancer and his visibly deteriorating body as powerful leverage in his mission. He was extraordinarily effective: the whole auditorium trembled when Sal, in a wheelchair, frozen in his cast, exhorted: "You want to destroy your body with nicotine or alcohol or heroin? You want to smash it up in autos? You're depressed and want to throw it off the Golden Gate Bridge? Then give me your body! Let me have it! I want it! I'll take it! I want to live!"

In his account of individuals who conquered cancer, Curtis Bill Pepper describes how a teen-age athlete confronted the amputation of his leg. After months of chemotherapy, losing his hair, throwing up in the car, he was at last in remission. Here is his conclusion: "I believe we the victors should help others coming after us. We should turn about and take three steps backward and pick up at least two people on their way out of the cancer concentration camp."

Perhaps it is the resilient captives I have studied—men and woman unscarred by seemingly endless terror and deprivation—who show most dramatically the healing power of compassion. While serving as U.S. Ambassador to Colombia in 1979, Diego Asencio, along with other diplomats, spent sixty-one excruciating days as a hostage of gun-wielding terrorists. "I think what helped most," he recalls, "was that I started working for the benefit of others." Asencio encouraged his fellow hostages, helped organize their routines, and took the lead in bargaining with the captors. "I wasn't just sitting in a corner. I was trying to take care of the other hostages, so I didn't have much of an opportunity to brood."

In the Vietnam prison camps, simple acts of charity toward one another helped to raise the captives' power of endurance. "The best thing you could do," says former POW Richard A. Stratton, "was to give when you had no hope of getting anything in return."

One powerful example is the story of Navy Lieutenant Porter Halyburton, a white southerner who found himself in a North Vietnamese prison cell with Air Force Major Fred V. Cherry, a black officer. When Cherry was shot down nine months earlier, his left arm, shoulder, and ankle were broken, but he received no medical attention. He became feverish, his shoulder infected, and the flesh around it decayed.

At first the two cell mates did not seem destined to become close. "Hally," a southerner, was shocked, Fred thought, to find himself jailed with a black man. But in the months that followed, Hally was to become Fred's salvation. He forced Fred to eat. He bathed him and carried him to the waste bucket. Despite the awful odor from Fred's left shoulder, Hally carefully tucked him into bed each night. And he talked to Fred constantly to keep his mind off his desperate physical agony.

Cherry owes his life to Halyburton, but as John G. Hubbell, author of *P. O. W.*, notes: "It works both ways. Acts of caring made the POWs feel better about themselves. It strengthened them immeasurably in their long ordeal."

During his nearly eight years as a POW in Vietnam, Air Force Colonel Robinson Risner became a special target of his captors. In order to disrupt the Americans' growing cohesiveness and organization, the Vietnamese guards locked Risner, the senior officer in the prison, into the stocks. Always an active man, Risner now suffered the excruciating anguish not only of being held in a small, dark cell but of having both legs immobilized in stocks. The experience was close to intolerable, and he wondered how he could hold on to his sanity.

Risner's response was to pray—but not for release from his own bondage. That would come in God's good time. Instead, he prayed for his family, for other POWs, even for his Vietnamese jailers—and, finally, for strength and wisdom for himself.

Often in Vietnam, according to former POW Stockdale, "compassion fairly seeped through the walls." POWs shared rather than hoarded food, boosted one another's morale, and helped one another in outwitting the captor or in planning escape attempts. As a result, these men survived their ordeal with surprisingly few scars. Stockdale, now at Stanford University's Hoover Institution, believes he emerged from his own eight years in captivity with one main idea: "You *are* your brother's keeper."

Everett Alvarez, among the earliest POWs taken in Vietnam, recently described to me the importance of compassionate acts toward fellow sufferers: "We felt it was especially critical to reach out to the person who had begun to withdraw and stay by himself," said Alvarez, "to pass him food if he was starving, medicine if he was sick, or messages of hope if he was depressed."

Such efforts, Alvarez maintains, undoubtedly blessed the givers even more than the receivers. His own acts of caring, he feels, were critical in helping him to survive the desolation of Vietnam captivity. "There was a period when I was held apart from the other POWs in a section of the prison containing only Vietnamese prisoners," he recalls. "Once a day the turnkey would let us out, a few at a time, into the courtyard that was immediately in front of our cells. There was a little bath out there where we were allowed to wash our clothes and bathe.

"The door of my cell contained a tiny pinhole, and if I looked through it, I could see a person standing ten feet away right in front of me in the courtyard. Apparently one of the Vietnamese prisoners knew about the pinhole because he would come and stand in front of it and wave and gesture at me. He would point at my clothes that I had left in the courtyard overnight to dry out and then point to his own rags.

"Now maybe he was putting me on. Maybe he was just a professional prison beggar, but I truly felt sorry for him. I had two pairs of trousers and two undershirts, and all he had was holes. So I arranged to leave him my extra clothing. When I saw how elated he became, it lifted my own spirits and helped me to go on."

Alvarez managed to share food with his unknown Vietnamese "comrade" as well. "I was being given rations that were better than his," he remembers. "The Vietnamese prisoners were getting only a pumpkin mush, while I was getting soup and a portion of bread. So I would give him half of my bread ration and whatever scraps of other food I could save.

"I know I didn't have to share with him. He wasn't a fellow POW. It was just instinctive on my part. But I must say that later, when I would look through the peephole and see him point to his stomach and smile, it made me feel awfully good inside."

Such acts by POWs, Alvarez feels, may have been motivated by moral or religious values for some; for others, by the need to be redeemed from an underlying sense of guilt; and for still others, it may have been a denial of their awful fate. The true dynamics may never be fully understood. In the end, however, it didn't really matter. "They were," says Alvarez, "acts of self-healing."

Even more remarkable displays of altruistic behavior and compassion toward fellow sufferers occurred in the Nazi death camps of the Second World War. Lucie Adelsberger, a psychologist who was imprisoned in Auschwitz-Birkenau, admits that in some people the camps produced a "relapse to the animal state." But she remembers quite different behavior as well among many other inmates: "Themselves already on the verge of starvation, they would sell their own bread ration in order to buy potatoes for a dying comrade, and thus give him a last happiness."

Elie Wiesel quotes a seasoned prisoner speaking to new arrivals: "We are all brothers, and we are all suffering the same fate. The same smoke floats over all our heads. Help one another. It is the only way to survive." A survivor of Treblinka describes life lived by that rule: "In our group we shared everything; and the moment one of the group ate something without sharing it, we knew it was the beginning of the end for him." In the moving Auschwitz diaries of Etty Hillesum, there is this final entry: "We should be willing to act as a balm for all wounds."

One survivor, when asked how it is that his experiences during the war had not embittered him, said that he learned the true meaning of friendship in Auschwitz. "When I was a child, strangers shielded me with their bodies from the blowing winds, for they had nothing else to offer but themselves." Children, too, revealed their compassionate instincts in the abyss of the Holocaust. Survivor Gerta Weissman recently reminisced about a friend named Ilse: "I remember one morning she found a raspberry in the gutter on the way to the factory. She carried it in her pocket all day long—it was a hot, hot day—to present it to me that night on a leaf that she plucked through the barbed wire. Her total possession became one raspberry, slightly mushed, with a little bit of dust on it. She never tasted another raspberry again. She died in my arms on a wet meadow in Czechoslovakia on a death march. She was eighteen years old."

In his book *The Survivor*, Terrence Des Pres summarizes the evidence: ". . . the testimony of survivors is full of examples of help—men and women giving a vital part of themselves, literally their last reserves, to keep each other going." The instinct for compassion in the face of crisis is clearly present in all of us, even in the face of the most severe trauma the mind can imagine.

Yet when we confront our own daily troubles, thinking of others does not always come easily. Indeed, for many people, self-absorption and self-pity become chronic responses to stress. The reason lies largely, I am convinced, in the passion our society has developed for self-service and self-love.

Escaping the Narcissism Trap

According to the ancient Greek legend, Narcissus was a beautiful young man who fell in love with his own reflection in a pool— so much so that he remained there until he died. His name has been given to the trait known as narcissism—or self-love—which can be seen in extreme form in the narcissistic personality. Such people have an inflated sense of their own importance. They feel entitled to everything, and they use others for their own purposes, offering nothing in return.

Narcissism is becoming increasingly common and accepted in our culture. Thinking of others is out of fashion now. Many forms of psychotherapy teach self-love as our most important responsibility, and compassion as a cop-out. Carl Rogers, the founder of so-called humanistic therapy, wrote that "the only question which matters is, 'Am I living in a way which is deeply satisfying to me, and which truly expresses me?' " Books intended to teach us how to make sure we never take second place— how to get everything we want out of life at any cost—become best-sellers: *Looking Out for Number One* or *The Art of Being Selfish*. Such books are, in effect, blueprints for the development of a narcissistic personality.

Evidence that we are not by nature self-serving and without compassion continues to mount. For many years, psychologists believed that we were born selfish, with an insatiable need to satisfy our own needs at the expense of those of others. Only slowly, Freud taught, can children be "socialized," and begin at least to act as if they care about others around them.

Today that dismal view of childhood has changed, with a host of studies showing that our young come into the world with a talent for kindness—a readiness to help others in trouble. Indeed, it seems clear that children display evidence of compassion and generosity virtually at the beginning of life. It may well be that it is the adult world—with its relentless and brutal "me first" philosophy—that subverts our early instincts.

In *The Culture of Narcissism* Christopher Lasch writes: "Having no hope of improving their lives in any ways that matter, people have convinced themselves that what matters is psychic self-improvement: getting in touch with their feelings, eating health food, taking lessons in ballet or belly-dancing. . . . To live for the moment is the prevailing passion—to live for yourself, not for your predecessors or posterity. . . ."

Too many people in America, Frankl recently observed, respond enthusiastically to our self-serving culture. "You're always forced—ordered—to feel joy, be happy, and experience pleasure," says Frankl. Self-sacrifice and thinking about others are made to seem irrelevant, even unhealthy. As a result, many of us are left with little capacity to practice empathy and compassion in our daily lives—let alone in the face of crisis.

Not that self-interest can be totally suppressed when crises occur. It's natural enough to withdraw into ourselves when we've been hurt. During the period immediately following a stressful experience, studies show, we want most of all to make ourselves feel better, and we just don't have the energy for other people. We want to think about our problems, not theirs.

Yet, ironically, helping others is eventually the best thing we can do for ourselves. As psychologists Michael and Lise Wallach have observed, today's narcissistic gospel "often leads people away from the sources of happiness and satisfaction they so desperately seek." If rumination and self-involvement become a habit, feelings toward others are deadened, and communication and contact wither. We end up losing the very human ties we require to sustain ourselves in times of greatest need. "To live without feeling sympathy," wrote Samuel Johnson, "or afflicted without tasting the balm of pity, is a state more gloomy than solitude: it is not retreat, but exclusion from mankind."

Moreover, in turning inward, we risk becoming professional victims, driving others further away. We've all met such people. They are totally obsessed with themselves and with the raw deal that life has dealt them. "Chronic kvetches," my mother used to call them—people who wear the battle scars of life as if they were badges of honor and use them promiscuously as excuses for self-serving and selfish behavior.

Barbara Gordon recently described how she reacted when, on her road back from emotional collapse, friends would call to make contact with her. "Time and again," she writes, "I would end the conversation abruptly. I was then still too locked in sadness, in the ungenerosity of self-concern, to give a damn about others' lives. . . . My questions about husbands, wives, jobs, lovers, children, were perfunctory, performed by rote. Like a plant deprived of sunlight and water, I could not blossom—for myself or anyone else."

Eventually, however, Barbara learned what it takes to begin life again as a victor rather than a victim. And she wanted to teach what she learned to others. "We ought to have courses on starting over," she says. "Our high schools are teaching subjects of far less importance. In my fantasy, thousands of students would be taught that self-absorption—the sort of narcissism so prevalent in the 1970s and 1980s—is also a powerful component of professional victimhood. It is especially during life's grimmest moments, they would be told, that you must force yourself to become interested in the lives of others. After a while, it will become a reflex."

A few years ago, Sandra Rosen was one of the hostages of the Hanafi Muslim takeover of the B'nai Brith Building in Washington, D.C. In the hours following her capture, Sandra found herself mired in self-pity. Hadn't she suffered enough? During the previous twenty years, she had endured sixteen operations, and her health had only recently begun to mend. Now her son was preparing to enter college, and she was planning a surprise party for her daughter, who was about to be confirmed in the Jewish faith. Convinced that she would never see her children again, Sandra began to cry.

Then, looking about, Sandra realized that her emotional display was demoralizing to those around her. Controlling her sobs, she vowed not to think only of herself and her family. By considering the feelings of others, Sandra reported after her release, she found it easier to continue. Years later, in her Iranian cell, hostage Katherine Koob made the same discovery. She prayed daily, "trying always to remember that there were a lot of people in the world a lot worse off than I was."

Sure, it's hard to overcome the impulse for self-interest, for nursing your own wounds, when you are hurting badly. But it's the only way your wounds will ever heal completely. Barbara Gordon has described how the process felt to her. "People began to matter," she writes. "As new people moved into the orbit of my life, my wariness and self-concern fell away. I was becoming interested in the lives of others—*their* loves and pains, *their* dreams and fears. No longer a hurting infant, I gave up my passivity and began to reach out to the world. I don't know the exact moment it happened. I'm only thankful that it happened."

Sometimes the transformation takes place with dramatic speed when we find that we are also suddenly consumed by a special mission.

A Cause to Live For

My father died on the Sabbath, his weekly hallowed day of rest. His life, begun in the perfumed air of Safed, Israel, ended eighty-four years later in a tiny hospital room on Long Island. Following Orthodox custom, the family members present spent the Sabbath in worship and study. Only when darkness fell did we begin the melancholy task of calling other family and friends to inform them of my father's death and of the funeral ceremony planned the following day, Sunday, at noon.

Long before evening, however, I began to wrestle with a dilemma. My brother Jack, fast losing his struggle with leukemia, was in the last months of his own life. In Detroit, on that very Sunday night, the congregation he had served as rabbi for thirty-five years was preparing to celebrate his extraordinary life and career with a testimonial dinner. This was to be the last public hurrah from the community my brother loved and served so passionately.

What to do? Tell Jack of his father's death? Despite his failing health, he would surely insist on attending the funeral, aborting the celebration to be given in his honor. Jack would return home to the rituals of "shiva"—the seven-day period of housebound mourning—and not to the sound of joyous and nourishing toasts of affection. Only if he didn't know the truth could the celebration in his honor go on as planned.

But keep the news from my brother? Not tell him that his father was dead? When the party was over would he understand that we did it for him—and for his cherished community?

The decision was made on Saturday night in telephone discussions with Jack's wife and with the organizer of the event. The celebration would go on. Jack would be told by me of our father's death only after the last guest had departed.

The scenario could unfold as planned, however, only if I carried out what at first seemed an impossible mission. Immediately after my father's funeral, I would have to board a plane for Detroit, arriving just in time for the late-afternoon cocktails that were to begin the celebration. Moreover, as I had gladly promised months earlier, as the evening's representative of the Segal family, I would be among the after-dinner speakers.

Out of the question, I thought. How could I say good-bye to my father, weep for his soul, watch his coffin disappear, and then, two hours later, drink a toast, pose for pictures, and regale an audience of 800 celebrants? How could I bare what was in my heart for my brother when my heart had been so freshly broken?

My doubts were short-lived. Of course, I could do it—and with surprising ease and zest. I could do it because I wanted to demonstrate the compassion I felt for my brother. And in doing so, I was liberated from my immobilizing melancholy and self-doubt.

I left the funeral in Long Beach and flew to Detroit. I embraced my brother and smoothly parried his questions about our father's health. I drank champagne, made small talk with Jack's congregants, took my place at the head table, and, when my turn came, spoke without strain about the guest of honor, the hero of my childhood. I recounted vignettes of Jack's life, and, looking down at his sunken but radiant face, his eyes fixed on mine, I told the throng of my undying love for him. Then, when it was all over, the two of us sat in the quiet of his study. I held my brother's hand and told him that our father was dead—and we cried together.

I have recounted this event because it highlights an invaluable lesson: The pain we feel, the losses we sustain, become infinitely more bearable when we adopt a mission of caring. The dual grief I faced—the fresh death of my father and the slow dying of my brother—became infinitely more manageable because I had turned outward. Devotion to a cause had muted my impulses for rumination, self-absorption, and self-pity—not only during that momentous day but in the trying months I still faced.

Sometimes, as in my case, we can pursue a cause that is embodied in a single person—a relative, a dear friend, a cherished colleague. At other times, we can give ourselves over to a group, or even to masses of people who remain unseen. Consider, for example, the case of Jack Hinckley.

It has been more than three years since John Hinckley, Jr., who was described in the press as a "well-off dropout," fired six Devastator bullets from a .22-caliber pistol into President Reagan and three others, including presidential aide James Brady. For John's father, Jack, this tragedy might have meant the end of the road. Here he was, oil executive and self-made millionaire, conservative Republican, faithful churchgoer, loving husband and family head—and now the shocked and stigmatized father of an attempted assassin.

Today the lives of Jack Hinckley and his wife, JoAnn, have changed dramatically. Aware of his failure to recognize how sick his son was, he has turned his life over to helping others escape a similar fate. Hinckley has resigned as president of Vanderbilt Energy Corporation, turning the company he founded in 1970 over to his elder son, Scott. He and JoAnn have left their comfortable Colorado home and moved to a two-bedroom apartment with leased furniture in McLean, Virginia. There they can be near their younger son and devote their considerable energies to the American Mental Health Fund, an organization they founded last year. Working out of a tiny office in McLean donated by a friend, Jack Hinckley gives lectures, raises money—and tries to offer help to other families facing the specter of mental illness.

His organization has already accumulated $200,000 from the Hinckleys' savings, donations, and fees Jack has earned. That sum is small, but Hinckley nevertheless looks ahead to a massive public-education campaign about mental health. "We're trying to publicize the warning signals of mental illness so other families can see them where we didn't," he says. "We want to bring mental illness out of the closet."

"I think that at this time in my life, I could have done a thousand things that I would have enjoyed more," he told me. "But I know in my guts I'm doing the right thing. I can't think of anything more worthwhile than helping the mentally ill—and preventing needless suffering in the future. I decided to try to cause something good to come from John's illness and tragedy. We want to bring some joy and hope to those who are now hurting, and to prevent needless suffering for those yet to come."

The Hinckleys' daughter, Diane Sims, agrees: "If in some small way our experiences can help others, then that's the way it should be."

Many ordinary people less well known than Jack Hinckley have helped themselves to overcome their ordeal by finding a cause to work for. In Shakespeare's words, we can all "draw from the heart of suffering itself the means of inspiration and survival." Even children. One evening in April, 1979, four terrorists entered the Israeli coastal town of Nahariya from the sea in a motor-powered dinghy. They broke into the apartment of Danny and Semadar Heran, the young parents of two daughters—Einat, five, and Yael, two. They took Danny and Einat back to their dinghy on the beach and shot Danny dead. When the Israeli forces approached, they picked up little Einat by the feet and smashed her head open on a rock. Back at the apartment, Yael and her mother hid in a utility room. When Yael started to cry, the terrorized Semadar clamped her hand over the two-year-old's mouth so hard that she inadvertently suffocated her own child.

Twelve-year-old Hadara Minster was the Haran's baby-sitter when the attack occurred. As reported by Roger Rosenblatt in *Children of War*, she withdrew completely after the incident. She refused to talk with anyone, would not go to school, and eventually would not even leave her home. A poem she wrote captured her feeling of hopelessness.

> If there is a God
> How does this happen?
> Who even needs it?
> Let's get it over with.
> Let's finish this matter.

Eventually, however, Hadara dramatically pulled herself out of her immobilizing melancholy. The turning point came when she organized a peace conference between Arab and Jewish children in her school. She called her meeting "to bring the hearts closer."

At the State University of New York, Lynn Videka-Sherman studied nearly 200 patients after they had lost a child. Her results showed significantly less depression among parents who reinvested their energies in another person or activity. Some of them, for example, volunteered to help other parents who were facing the death of a child, in organizations like Compassionate Friends, a national self-help group that provides support to bereaved parents.

Indeed, an important ingredient in the success of many self-help groups, according to Yalom, is the act of helping one another: "Unlike individual counseling, in which the counselee is a passive recipient, the group provides an opportunity for members to give as well as to receive. Seeing themselves contribute to others' well-being enhances a sense of worth and value and reduces feelings of powerlessness and hopelessness."

The underlying mechanism of support that operates in groups of patients with advanced cancer is altruism, says Yalom. Patients who feel helpless and demoralized learn that they can be enormously useful to others. Thomas Jefferson would not be surprised. "Who, then, can so softly bind up the wound of another," he asked, "as he who has felt the same wound himself?"

Evangeline Bruce is the widow of diplomat David K. E. Bruce, who was an ambassador to West Germany and Britain, and the first American liaison chief in Peking in 1973. On the champagne and caviar circuit, Mrs. Bruce is known as an international hostess who entertains flawlessly. But in Washington circles she is also known as the founder of Sasha Bruce Youthwork Inc., a network of shelters and outreach programs for young people that focus on runaways and teen-agers with problems. "We are the only place in the District where people can walk in off the streets twenty-four hours a day without a referral," Mrs. Bruce says.

Nearly eight years ago, Mrs. Bruce's daughter Alexandra, or "Sasha," was shot to death by her husband on the family estate in Virginia. She was twenty-eight years old.

"After my daughter died, I wanted to see if there wasn't something that we could do as a memorial to her that would approximate in some way the work she had been interested in when she was at Radcliffe," Mrs. Bruce said. Sasha had worked for the Harvard student social-service agency.

Sasha Bruce Youthwork Inc., which worked with 586 teen-agers last year, now operates five programs, including a youth employment agency and a counseling and legal assistance program. "For me this work is a way of giving to something that

Sasha very much cared about," Mrs. Bruce told an interviewer. "I think this network for young people would have made her very happy. Of all the things I think she would have chosen, it would have been this."

To one degree or another, a compassionate investment in others is possible for all of us. As I write this book, a dear friend, Anne, is recovering from a searing loss. Just a few months ago, her beloved husband, Josh, died after a long struggle with pancreatic cancer. Anne sought out the help of a hospice program, which enabled the dying patient to spend the last days of his life in the warm and familiar environment of his own home—his life-support needs met by the efforts of a caring hospice staff.

Soon after Josh died, Anne began training for work in a hospice program. She is filling the void in her life by helping others as her own husband was helped. Anne has also joined a synagogue group known as the chevra kadisha (the holy fellowship), whose task is one of the most valued in all of Judaic tradition: to assist the bereaved in the first flush of their loss. Anne now serves others with behind-the-scene funeral tasks—sitting watch over the body, as tradition requires, and even helping to wash and clothe the corpse in the approved, ritualistic fashion.

Psychoanalysts might well label Anne's behavior a classic example of reaction formation—as an *over*compensation for the anxiety provoked by her loss. And some social psychologists might argue that such altruism is actually the mirror image of hedonism—an exercise in self-gratification. No matter. What counts is that she is being palpably healed by acts of compassion.

"Ugly facts," wrote Henry S. Haskins, "are a challenge to beautify them." To survive under stress, we must accept the challenge to turn outward and beautify the lives of others. For many of us, those others may well turn out to be the children in our midst.

Gaining Strength by Giving Strength to the Young

On any modern-day stress scale, my parents and their contemporaries would have gone over the top. Impoverished immigrants to a new land, unfamiliar with the language and customs, they faced new and seemingly insuperable challenges each day.

My father was a case in point. His life was filled with chronic uncertainties that many contemporary men might find unmanageable. Married at sixteen and the father of three at twenty, he moved with soul-wrenching speed from being a scribe and scholar into a new world as wage earner and maker of the good life in an alien land. For everyone else, it seemed, America was ablaze with opportunities. For so many others, my mother was quick to remind him, those opportunities were golden; but for the Segals, tin at best. His yearning for a more secure life for himself and his family were never requited.

It seems to me in retrospect that this man never stopped looking back from the soot-laden hills of eastern Pennsylvania to his childhood in the clear air of northern Galilee, from the world of work-for wages to the scholarly life he forsook as a teen-aged husband and father in ancient Jerusalem. Here was a biblical scholar who had committed to memory the Old Testament and its rabbinic commentaries now struggling to explain the advantages of a twenty-year endowment policy to the grocer around the corner. As a ten-year-old with a better command of English than he could muster, I often sat at the dining room table filling out his client's insurance application forms as he dictated them, aware of the melancholy yet resolute face over my shoulder.

How did my father survive?

I am convinced that the terrifying quicksand on which he walked turned to bedrock primarily because of his commitment to his children. He had a clear mission: to make a path for the

next generation. It was because of "de teiereh kinder" (the precious children) that his chaotic universe somehow became coherent and whole. We kids were the cause he lived for, and that
made all else possible.

The kind of strength my father drew from his role as a parent
can be ours as well. For us, too, an investment in the world of
the young can serve as a potent antidote to stress. A passionate
commitment to the children in our midst—the kind of commitment that places the child's interests above our present ones—
can help to blunt the anguish of our own disappointments and
frustrations. And in helping ourselves, we also help the young
to deal with the stresses they inevitably encounter in their own
lives.

Serving as a Model

We tend to look back longingly to childhood as a period free of
troubles. The truth is that childhood as a time of undiluted
pleasures is a fiction concocted by adults. The writer E. B. White
poignantly captured the universality of childhood stress:

> I was uneasy about practically everything; the uncertainty of
> the future; the dark of the attic; the panoply and discipline of
> school, the transitoriness of life, the mystery of church and
> God, the frailty of the body, the sadness of afternoon, the
> shadow of sex, the distant challenge of love and marriage, the
> far-off problem of livelihood. I brooded with them all . . .

All children are touched by similar fears and bewilderments,
wants unfulfilled, needs unmet. Apparently innocuous episodes
may wound the soul of a child—a sudden and inexplicable leave-
taking, the angry voices of parents overheard from the adjoining
bedroom, a teacher's slight. Such experiences are common to
children of all races and in all places.

For millions of children, however, such everyday hurts are the least of their problems. They confront stresses at least as intense as those we experience as adults. Psychologist Norman Garmezy and psychiatrist Michael Rutter regard childhood encounters with loss as "among the most distressing events virtually all humans, irrespective of age, are likely to experience." Sometimes the loss is obvious: the death of a parent or grandparent, unrelenting neglect or abuse by uncaring parents or surrogates, repeated separations through illness, hospitalizations, or family strife.

Sometimes, however, the sources of a child's hurts are less apparent: the departure of a friend, the disappearance of a favorite pet, a string of poor grades, cruel taunts on the playground, the continuing rejection by a Little League coach. "Children's griefs are little, certainly," wrote the poet, Percy Bysshe Shelley, "but so is the child. . . ."

The poet's insight was validated a few years ago in a study by psychologist Kaoru Yamamoto. He asked fourth-, fifth-, and sixth-graders to rate twenty life events on a seven-point scale. The children's judgments differed dramatically from those expected of an adult. Especially traumatic, they said, were such "little" griefs as "a poor report card," "being ridiculed in class," or "being picked last on a team." These are the kinds of "gashes," as Shelley termed them, that may well be felt as amputations by young children.

Caring adults will look below the surface of apparent serenity to the tides of psychological pain that children face in their daily lives, and will face in the future. The result is likely to be a healing sense of commitment to the young.

Often, of course—but far from always—that commitment flows from mother or father. Gloria Johnson Powell, now director of the Child Outpatient Department at the UCLA Neuropsychiatric Institute, recalls her childhood as one of five fatherless children of a black family living in Roxbury, Massachusetts. "Everything my mother did and said somehow got the message across that somehow we would succeed eventually," says Gloria, "no matter how tough things were for us at the moment."

From the tenements of New York's East Side and Brooklyn a half century ago came impoverished and bewildered immigrants whose children grew to be among the brightest lights on the American scene—writers, scientists, entertainers, politicians—men and women who made enduring contributions to society. Their capacity to look beyond today's trials to tomorrow's triumphs was learned from parents who saw their children as their reason for being. They were members of a generation of parents who would die for their children—protect them and love them with a love more fierce than the love of life itself—and their stance strengthened them in their struggles.

This kind of commitment is by no means a relic·of bygone days. Consider the case of Anna Hollis, a black mother of five boys. Eight months after she and her husband, Thomas, bought a Burger King franchise in Washington, he was shot and killed in an exchange of gunfire with an armed robber. The shooting left Anna with her five young sons to support and a shattered dream of independence and success.

Today, at age forty, Anna has realized that dream. Not only did she take over the restaurant where her husband died, but she now owns a second one. Although she had worked part time for her husband, she knew nothing about the business. But she learned it all during the long hours in which she did everything from cleaning stoves to analyzing balance sheets.

Anna fought and won her battle, she says, to make sure her sons got a good start in life. She wanted to be their model of what perseverance and guts can accomplish—and indeed four of the boys are now either in college or already working independently. In showing her sons the way, Anna herself was strengthened.

But an ennobling commitment to the young is hardly reserved for parents. In a surprising number of cases, children find sources of strength in someone other than Mom or Dad—a member of the extended family, or someone outside it. Grandparents, for example, often find renewed strength by lending strength to children growing up in a stress-filled environment. Or the key person might be an uncle or aunt, a playmate's parent, a physician, coach, clergyman—anyone who communicates protection, devotion, and compassion.

In the case of Sandra, born in poverty and raised in violence, it was an aunt who turned the tide—for herself as well as for the child. Sandra endured the death of two older sisters, the bitter separation and divorce of her parents, and a series of illnesses that had seriously threatened her life. In one of the foster homes where she lived, she was physically abused and neglected. By all the usual criteria, Sandra should have become a psychological casualty. In fact, the opposite is true. She is today a motivated teen-ager who enjoys close friends and is zestfully planning a college career. How did Sandra get that way?

Sandra's strength came largely from the influence of a single caring person, one vital anchor in a sea of stress. Her aunt, newly arrived in this country, had been widowed two years earlier. Without children of her own, without roots or moorings, she lavished on Sandra all of the compassion and commitment that lay dormant and unfulfilled within her. She took the child in and surrounded her with a precious blend of encouragement and caring. The resulting bond between these two human beings has transformed both their lives.

For many children, it is a teacher who turns the tide from defeat to victory. Consider the case of Uvaldo Palomares, a thoroughly overlooked member of a desperately poor migrant family. He ricocheted from one school to another, leaving a record of chronic failure that made administrators consider placing him in a class for the mentally retarded.

One day during his third year of repeating the second grade, a teacher watched him win all of the marbles in a playground game. When it was over, she sat down beside him. "You know, Uvaldo," she said, "any kid who is smart enough to play marbles as well as you do is smart enough to learn to read. Now you are going to learn to read." So she began to teach him.

Uvaldo's feelings about himself changed. He vividly remembers the exhiliration he felt at having a teacher who was convinced he could learn. She had taken hold of him—and she was not about to let go until he realized her expectations. Uvaldo is now a successful psychologist, saved from a wasted life by an adult who really cared—and who freely showed it. That woman's dedication to Uvaldo undoubtedly brought her the sense of fulfillment Henry Adams had in mind when he observed that "a teacher can affect eternity."

In my own childhood, it was an older brother—himself struggling with the Depression-era tasks of breaking away from home, finding work, and launching a career—who found strength in the strength he offered me.

When I was around twelve, I was overcome by a gnawing sense of weakness and failure. A cloud of apprehension hung over my life, and I lived in envy of the zest and energy of my peers. A perceptive psychologist would have been able to identify the dark and pervasive themes of my preadolescent years—hypochondria, terror of authority figures, anticipation of death.

My parents, with old-world ways, tried hard but could not help. My complaints of "funny feelings," of dizzy spells and shortness of breath, of imminent polio and meningitis, led me to the only source of healing they knew—their revered doctor.

Dr. Halpert, a stern and forbidding figure, hardly spoke to me. As he jabbed for the vein in my skinny arm, he offered parables of the ancient rabbis to my worshipful father. A few days later came the long-awaited verdict: "Gezunt aber mishugeh" (healthy but crazy). And he warned me to cast aside my crazy ways and give "nachas" (pleasure), not "tzorus" (troubles) to my parents.

In that difficult time, my brother Jack, a dozen years older than I, became my beacon for growth. It was Jack who guided me through the shoals of adolescence and into the open waters of adulthood, offering me the precious blend of strength and availability, the unmistakable messages of caring and commitment I so needed.

Jack wasn't around much. After he graduated from high school he left home without a penny for college in New York City. Although he was only a three-hour Lackawanna Railroad ride away, he might as well have been in Tibet. Imprisoned by my anxieties into a three-square-block childhood, New York seemed an exotic, faraway territory, a land flowing with lectures and concerts and the theatre, whose richness I could possess only through the accounts of my big brother. It now seems clear to me that his stories—the possibilities they suggested—recemented my psyche every time we met. If he could do it, couldn't I? Wasn't he, after all, my brother, and didn't he love me and believe in me?

I can still savor the anticipation that swelled in me as holiday time, and Jack's return, approached. To me it was symbolic of Jack's surpassing competence that he would arrive from the railroad station in a taxi. No bus or trolley car for him, no ride begged by phone from a neighbor. The sight of that taxi, its door half open, its smiling, confident passenger paying his fare while talking, always talking, was to my young eyes the ultimate vision of what adulthood and freedom could be. Seeing him alight

121

from the taxi, I would hurtle through the front door across the tiny porch, down the steps, and into his arms. That house and that street are gone, my brother is dead, and I am middle-aged. Yet the tableau nurtures me still: my smiling big brother, his briefcase and satchel dropped at his sides, his arms flung open, my eager face pressed against his.

Years later, when I was grown, I learned from Jack how troubled he himself was at the time he took me under his wing. His emotional investment in me had helped to sustain him as he struggled to "make it" in the big city, and had increased his own zest and confidence in his ability to deal with the hard times and frustrations that confronted him.

All of the adults I have described—Sandra's aunt, Uvaldo's teacher, my own brother—were acting as powerful models for children floundering in a sea of stress. Contemporary psychologists agree that children learn many of their most important values and attitudes by observing the behavior of the adults around them.

What a powerful source of motivation and strength this offers us! How we respond to the crises in our own lives will help to shape our children's response to theirs. If we live scared, so will they. And if we show courage and resolve, they will do the same. The realization that we are the templates for our children's lives should embolden us in dealing with the crises in our lives. "The idea of being a model for others, especially for one's children," writes Yalom, ". . . can fill life with meaning until the moment of death."

This turns out to be possible even in the midst of the harshest experiences. Lisa Vice, now thirty-three, endured seemingly endless years of deprivation and despair. As an adolescent, she walked the streets of New York barefoot, panhandled, and slept on rooftops. At seventeen, she became pregnant by a man who left her after he learned she was going to have a child. A year later, she was already a high school dropout, an unwed mother, a welfare recipient.

Then Lisa started her climb back. She took part-time jobs, mainly cleaning apartments and office buildings, and trained as a secretary. She took several adult education courses, and then, in 1981, enrolled full time in Hunter College. Not long ago, the newspapers reported the standing ovation she received at her graduation ceremonies in Madison Square Garden. Lisa finished her degree with grades high enough to allow her to be a member of Phi Beta Kappa. Soon she will begin teaching remedial English to high school dropouts in Brooklyn, while working toward a master's degree. Looking back, Lisa says it was her daughter, Zoe, now fifteen, who helped her to get through her long struggle. "I was so depressed that if I hadn't had her, I think I might have gone the suicide route," she admits. "But there was no one else to care for my child."

Viktor Frankl would understand Lisa's commitment. He has described how, during his years as a concentration camp inmate, he was able to deter a number of fellow prisoners from suicide by reminding them of their responsibility to their children, who were being kept safely in hiding outside.

For countless adults today, an abiding concern for the child's welfare might well hold the key to dealing successfully with the stresses besetting them. A passionate commitment to our children—the kind that places the child's future interests above our own present ones—can help to blunt the anguish of our own disappointments and frustrations. And it can surely fortify the young as they prepare to deal with the stresses they will inevitably encounter in their own lives.

Each of us can gain strength from the knowledge that we project ourselves into the lives of future generations. Indeed, herein may lie the immortality for which we all yearn.

Some people look on any setback as the end.
They're always looking for the benediction
rather than the invocation. But you can't quit.
HUBERT H. HUMPHREY

Epilogue:
The Courage
to Prevail

An old story relates that a traveler in northern Vermont, convinced that he was on the wrong road, came to a halt in a village.

Calling one of the villagers to the car window, he said, "Friend, I need help. I'm lost."

The villager looked at him for a moment. "Do you know where you are?" he asked.

"Yes," said the traveler. "I saw the name of the village as I entered."

The man nodded his head. "Do you know where you want to be?"

"Yes," the traveler replied, and named his destination. The villager looked away for a moment. "You ain't lost," he said at last, "you just need directions."

Emotionally speaking, many of us are in the position of that traveler. We know where we are—disappointed, grieved, filled with a sense of loss and remorse. And we know where we yearn to be—at peace, liberated from anguish and anxiety. Like the traveler, we are not permanently lost. We need directions.

This book was written to fill that need—to provide directions for those seeking the road back from the stress-filled crises of their lives.

During times of trouble, that road is often hard to find. To begin with, we tend at such times to lose all sense of what normal life and well-being are actually like. We begin to feel as if life were *always* shrouded in melancholy, and we are unable to conjure up memories of earlier, happier times. "I know that I used to have a good and contented life," a recently divorced neighbor said to me, "but I can't imagine even one moment of it." Mired in a crisis, many of us similarly find that we are unable to recapture even in our minds those periods when the world was graced with buoyancy and enthusiasm instead of loathing and dread.

Second, persons traumatized by crises feel cut off not only from the past but from the future as well. The days ahead loom without promise; the outlook is bleak, filled only with foreboding. As one recent widower told me: "I am dead inside . . . I must always awaken to the dullness and misery of it all. My future has disappeared." It is difficult indeed to convince such an individual that life can become precious again, filled with triumphant possibilities.

To rediscover the joys of the past and feel zest for the future once again, we desperately need an agenda for the present. We need directions for today. With them, the darkness can be pierced. Said the great Unitarian minister A. Powell Davies: "There is a light within each of us that need never entirely go out. We can lose the battles, but not the war. We can go on when our minds tell us that there is no point in going on—because something wiser than our intellectual knowledge, something deep inside tells us we *can* go on. And we do."

Communication. Taking control. Finding a purpose. Shedding guilt. Showing compassion.

It doesn't take much to apply the strategies presented in this book in the face of life's ordinary irritations and frustrations. But it takes a great deal, indeed, when you are mired in emotional pain and the heart is breaking. Yet in doing so, you will discover in yourself the courage that makes possible victory over even the severest stress.

Shlomo Breznitz has accurately defined the nature of such courage in the face of adversity: "It is when fear dictates 'run' and the mind dictates 'stay,' when the body dictates 'don't' and the soul dictates 'do' that the heroic battle is being waged. Life shrinks or expands in proportion to one's courage."

Those who have suffered and prevailed know the surprising fruits of victory over stress. In a remarkable number of cases, they find that after their ordeal they begin to operate at a higher level than ever before. Many enjoy life more. They become more productive, and their capacity for loving and accepting love is increased. "Always it is in the desert," wrote Davies, "that a highway is proclaimed; always it is the wilderness that is declared to blossom like the rose."

The terrible experiences of our lives, despite the pain they bring, can become our redemption. Life's crises can come to be our conquests.

References

INTRODUCTION

American Psychiatric Association. *Diagnostic and statistical manual of mental disorders*, 3d ed. Washington, D.C., 1980.

Caplan, G. *Principles of preventive psychiatry*. New York: Basic Books, 1964.

Edelstein, E. L. Reactivation of concentration camp experiences as a result of hospitalization. In C. D. Spielberger, I. G. Sarason, and N. A. Milgram, eds. *Stress and anxiety*, vol. 8. Washington, D.C.: Hemisphere Publishing, 1982.

Ellis, E. M., Atkeson, B. M., and Calhoun, K. S. An assessment of long-term reactions to rape. *Journal of Abnormal Psychology*, 1981, 90, 263–66.

Figley, C. R., and McCubbin, H. I., eds. *Stress and the family, vol. 2: coping with catastrophe*. New York: Brunner Mazel, 1983.

REFERENCES

Garmezy, N. Foreword. In Werner, E., and Smith, R. S. *Vulnerable but invincible.* New York: McGraw-Hill, 1982, xiii–xix.

Garmezy, N. Stressors of childhood. In N. Garmezy and M. Rutter, eds., *Stress, coping, and development in children.* New York: McGraw-Hill, 1983, 43–84.

Holmes, T. H., and Rahe, R. H. The social readjustment rating scale. *Journal of Psychosomatic Research,* 1967, 11, 213–218.

Kagan, J. Family experience and the child's development. *American Psychologist,* 1979, 34, 886–891.

Kaplan, G. *Principles of preventive psychiatry.* New York: Basic Books, 1964.

Luborsky, L., Docherty, J. P., and Penisk, S. Onset conditions for psychosomatic symptoms. *Psychosomatic Medicine,* 1973, 35, 187–201.

McGrath, J. E. The editor's page. *Journal of Social Issues,* 1983, 39, introductory pages not numbered.

Moos, R. H., ed. *Human adaptation: coping with life crises.* Lexington, Mass.: D. C. Heath and Co., 1976.

Moos, R. H., and Tsu, V. D. Human competence and coping: an overview. In R. H. Moos, ed. *Human adaptation: coping with life crises.* Lexington, Mass.: D. C. Heath and Co., 1976, 3-16

Murphy, L., and Moriarity, A. *Vulnerability, coping and growth from infancy to adolescence.* New Haven, Conn.: Yale University Press, 1976.

Perloff, L. S. Perceptions of vulnerability to victimization. *Journal of Social Issues,* 1983, 39, 41–62.

Rutter, M. Stress, coping, and development: some issues and some questions. In N. Garmezy and M. Rutter, eds. *Stress, coping, and development in children.* New York: McGraw-Hill, 1983.

Silver, R. L., and Wortman, C. B. Coping with undesirable life events. In J. Garber and M. E. P. Seligman, eds., *Human helplessness: Theory and applications*. New York: Academic Press, 1980.

Taylor, S. E., Wood, Joanne V., and Lichtman, R. R. It could be worse: selective evaluation as a response to victimization. *Journal of Social Issues*, 1983, 39, 19–40.

Turk, D. C. Factors influencing the adaptive process with chronic illness: Implications for intervention. In I. G. Sarason and C. D. Spielberger, eds. *Stress and anxiety, vol. 6*. Washington, D.C.: Hemisphere Publishing Corporation, 1979.

Weinfeld, M., Sigal, J. J., and Eaton, W. W. Long-term effects of the holocaust on selected social attitudes and behaviors of survivors: A cautionary note. *Social Forces*, 60, September 1981, 1–19.

Wills, T. A. Social comparison in coping and help-seeking. In B. M. DePaulo, A. Nadler, and J. D. Fisher, eds. *New directions in helping, vol. 2: help-seeking*. New York: Academic Press, 1982.

CHAPTER 1

Alvarez, E. The adaptation of and dependence on sound as experienced by American prisoners of war in Vietnam. Unpublished research paper. November 7, 1974.

Berkman, L. F., and Syms, S. L. Social networks, host resistance, and mortality: a nine-year follow-up study of Alameda County residents. *American Journal of Epidemiology*, 1979, 109, 186–204.

Bernikow, L. Alone: yearning for companionship in America. *New York Times Magazine*, August 15, 1982, 25–31.

Brown, G. W., Brochlain, M. N., and Harris, T. Social class and psychiatrist disturbance among women in an urban population. *Sociology*, 1975, 9, 225–254.

Caplan, G. *Support systems and community mental health*. New York: Behavioral Publications, 1974.

Caplan, G. Mastery of stress: Psychosocial aspects. *The American Journal of Psychiatry*, 138, April 1981, 413–420.

REFERENCES

Cassel, J. Psychosocial processes and "stress": theoretical formulations. *International Journal of Health Services*, 1974, 4, 471–482.

Coates, D., Wortman, C. B., and Abbey, A. Reactions to victims. In I. H. Frieze, D. Bar-Tal, and J. S. Carroll, eds. *New approaches to social problems*. San Francisco, Calif.: Jossey-Bass, 1979.

Coates, D., and Winston, T. Countering the deviance of depression: Peer support groups for victims. *Journal of Social Issues*, 1983, 39, 169–194.

Cobb, S. Social support as a mediator of life stress. *Psychosomatic Medicine*, 1976, 38, 300–310.

Cowan, E. Help is where you find it. *American Psychologist*, April 1982, 37, 385–395.

Deaton, J. E., et al. Coping activities in solitary confinement of U. S. Navy POWs in Vietnam. *Journal of Applied Social Psychology*, 1977, 7, 239–257.

Gartner, A. J., and Riessman, F. Self-help and mental health. *Hospital and Community Psychiatry*, August 1982, 33, 631–635.

Goleman, D. Confiding in others improves health. *The New York Times*, September 18, 1984, C-1.

Gordon, B. You can begin again. *Parade*, December 30, 1984, 4–6.

Gore, S. The effect of social support in moderating the health consequences of unemployment. *Journal of Health and Social Behavior*, 1978, 19, 157–165.

Greenblatt, M., Becerra, R. M., and Serafetinides, E. A. Social networks and mental health: an overview. *The American Journal of Psychiatry*, 139, August 1982, 977–984.

Helsing, K. L., Szklo, M., and Comstock, G. W. Factors associated with mortality after widowhood. *American Journal of Public Health*, 1981, 71, 802–809.

Hubbell, J. G. *P.O.W.: A definitive history of the American prisoner-of-war in Vietnam*. New York: Reader's Digest Press, 1976.

Koranyi, E. K. Psychodynamic theories of the 'survivor syndrome'. *Canadian Psychiatric Association Journal*, 1969, 14, 165–174.

Kushner, H. S. *When bad things happen to good people*. New York: Avon Books, 1981.

Leon, G. R., et al. Survivors of the holocaust and their children: Current status and adjustment. *Journal of Personality and Social Psychology*, 1981, 41, 503–516.

Levy, L. H. Self-help groups: Types and psychological processes. *Journal of Applied Behavioral Sciences*, 1976, 12, 310–323.

Lieberman, M. A., and Borman, L. D. The impact of self-help groups on widows' mental health. *National Reporter*, 1981, 4, 2–6.

Lowenthal, M. F., and Haven, C. Interaction and adaptation: intimacy as a critical variable. *American Sociological Review*, 1968, 33, 20–30.

Lynch, J. M. *The broken heart: the medical consequences of loneliness*. New York: Basic Books, 1977.

Martin, J. L. The effects of social support on psychological distress among Vietnam veterans and their peers. Paper presented to the annual meetings of the American Psychological Association, Washington, D. C., August 1982.

Murphy, C. Anxiety, depression afflict many refugees here, experts find. *The Washington Post*, January 6, 1985, B1.

Nuckolls, K. B., Cassel, J., and Caplan B. H. Psychosocial assets, life crisis, and the prognosis of pregnancy. *American Journal of Epidemiology*, 95, 1972, 431–441.

Ogg, E. *Partners in coping: groups for self and mutual help*. Public Affairs Pamphlet No. 559, Public Affairs Committee, New York City, 1978, 3.

Overstreet, H., and Overstreet, B. *The mind alive*. New York: Norton, 1954.

Pennebaker, J. W. Traumatic experience and psychosomatic disease: exploring the roles of behavioural inhibition, obsession, and confiding. *Canadian Psychology*, 1985, 26, 82–95.

President's Commission on Mental Health: Report of the task panel on community support systems. Washington, D.C.: U. S. Government Printing Office, 1978.

Riessman, F. Support groups as preventive intervention. Paper presented to Vermont Conference on Primary Prevention of Psychopathology. June 29, 1984, Burlington, Vermont.

Rodin, J. Applications to social problems. In G. Lindzey and E. Aronson, eds. *The handbook of social psychology*, vol. 3, 3rd ed. Reading, Mass.: Addison-Wesley, in press.

Rubenstein, C., and Shaver, P. Loneliness in two northeastern cities. In J. R. Hartog and Y. A. Cohen, eds. *The anatomy of loneliness*. New York: International Universities Press, 1980.

Peterson, K. S., and Stewart, S. A. The healing powers of family support. *USA Today*, November 29, 1984, 3D.

Rutledge, H. A. *In the presence of mine enemies*. Old Tappan, N. J.: Fleming H. Revell, 1973.

Schachter, S. *The psychology of affiliation*. Stanford, Calif.: Stanford University Press, 1959.

Segal, D. Soviet Jews: eyewitness report. *Near East Report*, June 15, 1984, 95.

Spiegel, D., Bloom, J. R., and Yalom, I. Group support for patients with metastatic cancer: a randomized prospective outcome study. *Archives of General Psychiatry*, May 1981, 38, 527–533.

U. S. Bureau of the Census. *Population characteristics*. Series P-20. No. 369, 1984.

Yalom, I. D. *The theory and practice of group psychotherapy*, 2d ed. New York: Basic Books, 1975.

CHAPTER 2

Altman, L. K. Hospital patients can suffer twice when staff adds insult to injuries. *The New York Times*, February 22, 1983, C–1.

Bandura, A. Self-efficacy. *Psychological Review*, 1977, 84, 191–215.

Bard, M., and Sangrey, D. *The crime victim's book*. New York: Basic Books, 1979.

Carroll, J. B., et al. A specific laboratory test for the diagnosis of melancholia: Standardization, validation, and clinical utility. *Archives of General Psychiatry*, 1981, 38, 15–22.

Deaton, J. E., et al. Coping activities in solitary confinement of U.S. Navy POWs in Vietnam. *Journal of Applied Social Psychology*, 1977, 7, 239–257.

Edel, L. ed. *The letters of Henry James, vol. 4: 1895–1916*. Cambridge, Mass.: The Belknap Press of Harvard University Press, 1984.

Ferretti, F. From the ashes of tragedy, self-help groups. *The New York Times*, June 4, 1984, B-12.

Fisher, K. Huntington's: knowledge can't erase the fear. *Monitor*, August 1984, 15, pp. 7–8.

Frankenhaeuser, M. Psychobiological aspects of life stress. In S. Levine and H. Ursin, eds. *Coping and health*. New York: Plenum Press, 1980.

Gartner, A., and Riessman, F. *Self-help in the human services*. San Francisco: Jossey-Bass, 1977.

Hall, E. A sense of control. *Psychology Today*, December 1984, 38–45.

Hanson, J. D., Larson, M. E., and Snowden, C. T. The effects of control over high intensity noise on plasma cortisol levels in rhesus monkeys. *Behavioral Biology*, 1976, 16, 333–340.

Heinemann, A. Victim for victims: The Theresa Saldana story. CBS telecast, November 12, 1984.

REFERENCES

Hiroto, D. S. Locus of control and learned helplessness. *Journal of Experimental Psychology*, 1974, 102, 187–193.

Kagan, J. Stress and coping in early development. In M. Rutter and N. Garmezy, eds. *Stress, coping, and development in children*. New York: McGraw-Hill, 1983, 191–216.

Maddi, S. R., and Kobasa, S. C. *The hardy executive: health under stress*. Homewood, Illinois: Dow Jones-Irwin, 1984.

Maier, S. F., Anderson, C., and Lieberman, D. A. Influence of control of shock on subsequent shock-elicited aggression. *Journal of Comparative and Physiological Psychology*, 1973, 85, 582–592.

Maier, S. F., Seligman, M. E. P., and Solomon, R. L. Pavlovian fear conditioning and learned helplessness. In B. A. Campbell and R. M. Church, eds. *Punishment and aversive behavior*. New York: Appleton-Century Crofts, 1969.

Pepper, C. B. *We the victors: Inspiring stories of people who conquered cancer and how they did it*. New York: Doubleday, 1984.

Pines, M. Psychological hardiness. *Psychology Today*, December 3, 1980, 34–44 + 98.

Prochnik, L. *Endings*. New York: Crown Publishers, 1980.

Rabin, D. Trapped in my body, I electronically escape. *Wall Street Journal*, January 27, 1984, 17.

Rabin, P. L. Credo for creeping paralysis. *Journal of the American Medical Association*. May 20, 1983, 249, 2649–2650.

Riessman, F. The "helper" therapy principle. *Social Work*, 1965, 10, 27–32.

Rodin, J. Managing the stress of aging: The role of control and coping. In S. Levine and H. Ursin, eds. *Coping and health*. New York: Plenum Press, 1980.

Rosenbaum, I. J. *The holocaust and halakhah*. New York: Ktav Publishing Co., 1976.

Rush, A. J., and Beck, A. T. Adults with affective disorders. In M. Hersen and A. S. Bellack, eds. *Behavior therapy in the psychiatric setting*. Baltimore: Williams and Wilkins, 1978.

Seligman, M. E. P. *Helplessness: On depression, development, and death*. San Francisco: W. H. Freeman and Co., 1975, 100.

Shales, T. The victim's own story. *The Washington Post*, November 12, 1984, C–1.

Snyder, B. Computer lets scientist speak, write, and work. *Nashville Banner*, May 31, 1983, 109, 1.

Taulbee, E. S., and Wright, H. W. A psycho-social behavioral model for therapeutic intervention. In C. D. Spielberger, ed. *Current topics in clinical and community psychology III*. New York: Academic Press, 1971, 92–125.

Weiss, J. M. Effects of coping responses on stress. *Journal of Comparative and Physiological Psychology*, 1968, 65, 251–260.

Yalom, I., and Greaves, C. Group therapy with the terminally ill. *American Journal of Psychiatry*, 1977, 13, 396–400.

Yalom, I. *Existential psychotherapy*. New York: Basic Books, 1980.

CHAPTER 3

Anatovsky, A. *Health, stress, and coping*. San Francisco: Jossey-Bass, 1980, 127.

Andreason, N. J. C., and Norris, A. S. Long-term adjustment and adaptation mechanisms in severely burned adults. *Journal of Nervous and Mental Disease*, 1972, 154, 352–362.

Beck, A. T. *Depression: causes and treatment*. Philadelphia: University of Pennsylvania Press, 1967.

Breznitz, S., ed. *Stress in Israel*. New York: Van Nostrand, 1983.

Camus, A. Cited in Jaffe, A. *The myth of meaning in the work of C. J. Jung*. London: Hodden and Stoughton, 1970, title page.

References

Chodoff, P., Friedman, S. B., and Hamburg, D. A. Stress, defenses, and coping behavior: Observations in parents of children with malignant disease. *American Journal of Psychiatry*, 1964, 120, 743–749.

Cornwell, J., Nurcombe, B., and Stevens, L. Family response to loss of a child by Sudden Infant Death Syndrome. *The Medical Journal of Australia*, 1977, 1, 656–658.

Doka, K. J., and Schwarz, E. Assigning blame: The restoration of "sentimental order" following an accidental death. *Omega*, 1978–79, 9, 279–285.

Douglas. W. O., ed. *The mind and faith of A. Powell Davies*. New York: Doubleday, 1959.

Dresner, S. H. *Levi Yitzhak of Berdichev: portrait of a hasidic master*. New York: Hartmore House, 1974.

Eitinger, L. Personal communication.

Eliach, Y. *Hasidic tales of the holocaust*. New York: Oxford University Press, 1982.

Frankl, V. E. *Man's search for meaning: An introduction to logotherapy*. New York: Washington Square, 1963, 121.

Gardner, J. Doctoral dissertation, University of Chicago, 1977.

Glick, I. O., Weiss, R. S., and Parkes, C. M. *The first year of bereavement*. New York: Wiley, 1974.

Gordon, B. You can begin again. *Parade*, December 30, 1984, pp. 4–6.

Helmrath, T. A., and Steinitz, E. M. Death of an infant: parental grieving and the failure of social support. *The Journal of Family Practice*, 1978, 6, 785–790.

Hobbs, N. Sources of gain in psychotherapy. *American Psychologist*, 1962, 17, 742–748.

Horowitz, M. J. *Stress response syndromes*. New York: Aronson, 1976.

138

Houghton, J. After the funny farm. *Schizophrenia Bulletin*, Department of Health and Human Services, Public Health Service, 6, 1980.

Hume, D. Cited in Nagel, T. *Mortal Questions*. London: Cambridge University Press, 1979, 20.

Jung. C. *Collected works: The practice of psychotherapy, vol. XVI.* New York: Pantheon Bollingen Series, 1966, 83.

Kastenbaum, P. The vitality of death. *Omega*, 1971, 2, 253–271.

Kleiman, D. A muscular dystrophy victim learns to help the mentally ill. *The New York Times*, August 3, 1984, B–1.

Klinger, E. *Meaning and void.* Minneapolis, Minn.: University of Minnesota Press, 1977.

Kubler-Ross, E. *Chicago Medicine*, 76, August 25, 1973, 661.

Maddi, S. The existential neurosis. *Journal of Abnormal Psychology*, 1967, 72, 311–325.

Mansfield, K. *Journal.* London: Constable, 1954.

National Public Radio. The will to live. Interview with Jacob Javits. *All Things Considered.* May 17, 1984.

National Public Radio. Nazi liberators and survivors. *All Things Considered.* April 17, 1985.

Neuberger, R. Cited in Frank, J. Nuclear death—the challenge of ethical religion. *The Ethical Platform*, April 29, 1962.

Prochnik, L. *Endings.* New York: Crown, 1980.

Samuels, E. Unpublished letter to Jack Segal, November 25, 1973.

Shanfield, S. B. On surviving cancer: Psychological considerations. *Comprehensive Psychiatry*, 1980, 21, 2, March/April, 1980. 128–134.

Schmitt, A. *Dialogue with Death.* Harrisonburg, Va.: Choice Books, 1976, 55–58.

Shneidman, E. S., and Farberow, N. L. A psychological approach to the study of suicide notes. In E. S. Shneidman, N. L. Farberow, and R. E. Litman, eds. *The psychology of suicide*. New York: Science House, 1970, 159–164.

Silver, R. L., Boon, C. and Stones, M. H. Searching for meaning in misfortune: making sense of incest. *Journal of Social Issues*, 1983, 2, 81–102.

Silver, R. L., and Wortman, C. B. Coping with undesirable life events. In J. Garber and M. E. P. Seligman, eds. *Human helplessness*. New York: Academic Press, 1980, 279–375.

Spinetta, J. J., Swarner, Joyce A., and Sheposh, J. P. Effective parental coping following the death of a child from cancer. *Journal of Pediatric Psychology*, 1981, 6, 251–263.

Szymusik, A. Personal communication.

Taylor, S. E. Adjustment to threatening events: A theory of cognitive adaptation. *American Psychologist*, November 1983, 38, 1161–1173.

Tolstoy, L. *My confession, my religion, the gospel in brief*. New York: Charles Scribner's Sons, 1929, 14.

Tsongas, P. *Heading home*. New York: Alfred A. Knopf, 1984.

Videka-Sherman, L. Coping with the death of a child: a study over time. *American Journal of Orthopsychiatry*, 1982, 52, 688–698.

Wolman, B. Principles of international psychotherapy. In *Psychotherapy: theory, research, and practice*, 1975, 12, 149–159.

Yalom, I. D. *Existential psychotherapy*. New York: Basic Books, 1980.

Yarom, N. Facing death in war—An existential crisis. In S. Breznitz, ed. *Stress in Israel*. New York: Van Nostrand, 1983, 3–38.

Wallerstein, J. S., and Kelley, J. B. *Surviving the breakup: How children and parents cope with divorce*. New York: Basic Books, 1980.

Wolfenstein, M. *Disaster: A psychological study*. Glencoe, Ill.: The Free Press, 1957.

CHAPTER 4

Abrams, A. A trial for the victim. *Newsday*, March 26, 1984, Part II, 4.

Ayalon, O. Coping with terrorism. In D. Meichenbaum and M. E. Jaremko, eds. *Stress reduction and prevention*. New York, Plenum, 1983.

Bard, M., and Sangrey, D. *The crime victim's book*. New York: Basic Books, 1979.

Berglas, S. Why did this happen to me? *Psychology Today*, February 1985, 44–48.

Bonoir, D. E., Champlin, S. M., and Kolly, T. S. *The Vietnam veteran: A history of neglect*. New York: Praeger, 1985.

Brickner, R. P. *My second twenty years: An unexpected life*. New York: Basic Books, 1976, 153.

Bulman, R. J., and Wortman, C. B. Attributions of blame and coping with the "real world": Severe accident victims react to their lot. *Journal of Personality and Social Psychology*, 1977, 35, 351–363.

Farina, A., Hagelauer, H. D., and Holzberg, J. D. The influence of psychiatric history on physicians' responses to a new patient. *Journal of Consulting and Clinical Psychology*, 1976, 44, 499.

Gaylin, W. *Feelings: Our vital signs*. New York: Harper and Row, 1979.

Goffman, E. *Stigma: notes on the management of spoiled identity*. Englewood Cliffs, N.J.: Prentice-Hall, 1963.

Goleman, D. To dream the impossible dream: An interview with Shlomo Breznitz. *American Health*, December 1984, 60–61.

Greer, S. Psychological responses to breast cancer and eight-year outcome. Paper presented at the annual meeting of the American Psychological Association, Los Angeles, Calif., August 1981.

Hendin, H., and Haas, A. P. *Wounds of war: The psychological aftermath of combat in Vietnam*. New York: Basic Books, 1985.

141

References

Janoff-Bulman, R. Characterological versus behavioral self-blame: Inquiries into depression and blame. *Journal of Personality and Social Psychology*, 1979, 37, 1798–1809.

Jones, et al. *Social stigma: The psychology of marked relationships*. New York: W. H. Freeman and Co., 1984.

Frieze, I. H. Perception of battered wives. In I. H. Frieze, D. Bar-Tal, and J. S. Carroll, eds. *New approaches to social problems: applications of attribution theory*. San Francisco: Jossey-Bass, Inc., 1979.

Huffine, C. L., and Clausen, J. A. Madness and work: short- and long-term effects of mental illness on occupational careers. *Social Forces*, 1979, 57, 1049–62.

Katz, I. *Stigma: A social psychological analysis*. Hillsdale, New Jersey: Lawrence Erlbaum Associates, 1981.

Kushner, H. S. *When bad things happen to good people*. New York: Schocken Books, 1981.

Lerner, M. J. The desire for justice and reactions to victims. In J. Macaulay and L. Berkowits, eds. *Altruism and helping behavior*. New York: Academic Press, 1970, p. 207.

Lerner, M. J. *The belief in a just world*. New York: Plenum, 1980.

Linscott, S. Are friends still friends in adversity? *The New York Times*, August 29, 1984.

Marcus, R. New Bedford rape case has sometimes cast accuser as accused. *The Washington Post*, March 4, 1984, p. A2.

Peterson, C., Schwartz, S. M., and Seligman, M. E. P. Self-blame and depressive symptoms. *Journal of Personality and Social Psychology*, 1981, 41, 253–259.

Peterson, C., and Seligman, M. E. P. Causal explanations as a risk factor in depression: Theory and evidence. *Psychological Review*, 1984, 91, 3, 347–374.

Petrillo, M., and Sanger, S. *Emotional care of hospitalized children: An environmental approach*. Philadelphia, Pa.: J. B. Lippincott Co., 1980.

Porter, C. *Blame, depression, and coping in battered women.* Unpublished doctoral dissertation. University of British Columbia, 1983.

Rabin, D., with Rabin, P. L., and Rabin, R. Occasional notes: Compounding the ordeal of ALS. *New England Journal of Medicine,* 37, August 19, 1982, 506–509.

Rabin, D., and Rabin, P. L. *To provide safe passage: The humanistic aspects of medicine.* New York: Philosophical Library, 1985.

Reader, E. C., Jr. Holding on to hope. In *Robins Reader.* Richmond, Va.: A. H. Robins Co.

Richlin, M., et al. Five-year medical followup of Vietnam POWs: Preliminary results. *U.S. Navy Medicine,* August 1980, 71, 19–28.

Ryan, William. *Blaming the victim.* New York: Pantheon, 1971.

Salasin, S. Caring for victims: An interview with Steven Sharfstein. *Evaluation and Change,* Special Issue, 1980, 18–20.

Satchell, M. Victims have rights too. *Parade Magazine,* March 17, 1985, 15–17.

Segal, J. Violent men—embattled women. *Cosmopolitan.* May 1976, 238–241.

Segal, J. *Captivity and beyond: Correlates of prisoner-of-war and hostage experiences.* Seminar presented at Center for Advanced Study in the Behavioral Sciences. Stanford, Calif., May 1980.

Schmalz, J. Crime victims seeking voice in legal system. *The New York Times,* March 6, 1985, B–2.

Symonds, M. Victims of violence: Psychological effects and aftereffects. *American Journal of Psychoanalysis,* 1975, 35.

Symonds, M. The "second injury" to victims. *Evaluation and Change,* Special Issue, 1980, 36–38.

Taylor, S. E., Wood, J. V., and Lichtman, R. R. It could be worse: Selective evaluation as a response to victimization. *Journal of Social Issues,* 1983, 39, pp. 19–40.

143

World Health Organization. *Schizophrenia: An international follow-up study*. New York: Wiley, 1979.

Wortman, C. B. Causal attributions and personal control. In J. H. Harvey, W. J. Ickes, and R. F. Kidd, eds. *New directions in attribution research*, Hillsdale N.J.: Erlbaum Associates, 1976.

CHAPTER 5

Adelsberger, L. *Auschwitz, ein Tatsachenbericht*. Berlin: Letner, 1956.

Ayalon, O. Children as hostages. *The Practitioner*, October 1982, 226, 1773–1781.

Baumann, D. J., Cialdini, R. B., and Kenrick, D. T. Altruism as hedonism: Helping and self-gratification as equivalent responses. *Journal of Personality and Social Psychology*, 1981, 40, 1039–1046.

Bellah, R. N., et al. *Habits of the heart: Individualism and commitment in American life*. Berkeley: University of California Press, 1985.

Des Pres, T. *The survivor*. New York: Simon and Schuster, 1976.

Eitinger, L. Denial in concentration camps: Some personal observations on the positive and negative functions of denial in extreme life situations. In S. Breznitz, ed. *The denial of stress*. New York: International Universities Press, Inc., 1984.

Gamarekian, B. Diplomat's widow aids the young. *The New York Times*, August 4, 1984.

Garmezy, N., and Nuechterlein, K. H. Invulnerable children: The fact and fiction of competence and disadvantage. *American Journal of Orthopsychiatry*, 1972, 42, 328–329 (Abstract).

Garmezy, N., and Rutter, M. Acute reactions to stress. In M. Rutter and L. Hersov, eds. *Child psychiatry: modern approaches, 2nd ed.* Oxford, England: Blackwell Scientific Publications, 1985, 152–175.

Gordon, B. You can begin again. *Parade*, December 30, 1984, 4–6.

Hammer, J., and Kraft, B. New hope, old anguish. *People*, March 19, 1984, pp. 26–27.

Hillesum, E. *An interrupted life: The diaries of Etty Hillesum, 1941–1943*. New York: Washington Square Press, 1981.

Hinckley, J., and Hinckley, J. A. *Breaking points*. Grand Rapids, Mich.: Chosen Books, 1985.

Hubbell, J. G. *P. O. W.: A definitive history of the American prisoner-of-war in Vietnam*. New York: Reader's Digest Press, 1976.

Johnson, S. Problems of parental narcissism. *New York Times*, February 4, 1985, p. 20.

Klemsrud, J. Top graduate's long way up. *The New York Times*, June 9, 1985.

Kraft, B. New hope, old anguish. *People*, March 19, 1984, 26–27.

Lasch, C. The culture of narcissism. *Bulletin of the Menninger Clinic*, 1980, 44, 426–440.

Lasch, C. *The culture of narcissim: American life in an age of diminishing expectations*. New York: Warner Books, 1979, 29–33.

Moskovitz, S. *Love despite hate: Child survivors of the holocaust and their adult lives*. New York: Schocken Books, 1983.

National Public Radio. Nazi liberators and survivors. *All Things Considered*. April 17, 1985.

Pepper, C. B. *We the victors: Inspiring stories of people who conquered cancer and how they did it*. New York: Doubleday and Co., 1984.

Petrillo, M., and Sanger, S. *Emotional care of hospitalized children: An environmental approach*. Philadelphia, Pa.: J. B. Lippincott Co., 1980.

Rosenblatt, R. *Children of war*. Garden City, N.Y.: Anchor Press, 1983.

Rutter, M. Protective factors in children's responses to stress and disadvantage. In M. W. Kent and J. E. Rolf, eds. *Social competence in children: primary prevention of psychopathology*, vol. 3. Hanover, N.H.: University Press of New England, 1979.

Segal, J., and Segal, Z. Children who beat the odds. *Ladies' Home Journal*, December 1984.

Segal, J., and Segal, Z. *Growing up smart and happy*. New York: McGraw-Hill, 1985.

Seligman, M. E. P., et al. Attributional style and depressive symptoms among children. *Journal of Abnormal Psychology*, 1984, 93, 235–238.

Videka-Sherman, L., Effects of participation in a self-help group for bereaved parents: Compassionate Friends. In L. D. Borman, et al. eds. *Helping people to help themselves: Self-help and prevention*. New York: Haworth Press, 1982, 69–77.

Wallach, M. A., and Wallach, L. *Psychology's sanction of selfishness*. New York: W. H. Freeman and Co., 1983.

Wallach, M. A., and Wallach, L. How psychology sanctions the cult of the self. *The Washington Monthly*, February 1985, pp. 46–53.

White, E. B. *Letters of E. B. White*. New York: Harper and Row, 1976.

Wolfenstein, M. *Disaster: A Psychological Study*. Glencoe, Ill.: The Free Press, 1957.

Yalom, I. *The theory and practice of group psychotherapy*. New York: Basic Books, 1975.

Yalom, I. *Existential psychotherapy*. New York: Basic Books, 1980.

Yamamoto, K. Children's ratings of the stressfulness of experiences. *Developmental Psychology*, 1979, 15, 581–582.

Zahn-Waxler, C., and Radke-Yarrow, M. The development of altruism: Alternative research strategies. In N. Eisenberg, ed. *The development of prosocial behavior*. New York: Academic Press, 1982, pp. 109–137.

EPILOGUE

Davies, A. P. *The temptation to be good.* New York: Farrar, Straus and Young, 1952.

Breznitz, S. The courage to care. Presented at conference on Faith in Humankind, Washington, D.C., 1984.

AUTHOR'S NOTE

Dr. David Rabin and Senator Jacob Javits, whose heroic battles with illness are described in Chapter 2, died after the completion of this book. Their inspiration—and therefore their victory—did not.

Index